KU-573-440

Emotion and Object

Emotion
and
Object

J.R.S. Wilson

Cambridge
at the University Press
1972

Published by the Syndics of the Cambridge University Press
Bentley House, 200 Euston Road, London NW1 2DB
American Branch: 32 East 57th Street, New York, N.Y.10022

© Cambridge University Press 1972

Library of Congress Catalogue Card Number: 76-179160

ISBN: 0 521 08450 4

Printed in Great Britain
by Western Printing Services Ltd,
Bristol

Contents

Preface

This book was written in the spring and summer of 1968, and submitted as a doctoral dissertation at the University of Cambridge. With its completion I left philosophy and descended to less aethereal regions. Learning, and now teaching, a new subject has meant that I have had to keep revision to a minimum, and have been unable to take account of recent additions to the literature. I hope that, despite this, some of the ideas contained here may be of use to those who persist in the struggle I have fled.

Nowhere is originality more difficult to assess than in philosophy. Some specific debts are easy to acknowledge, resulting as they do from the conscious borrowing of an account, or theory, or idea. I owe such debts to D. Davidson, for the account of singular causal statements outlined in Chapter II, and to H. P. Grice, for certain ideas which I use in Chapter XVIII, and for the method of approach which governs that and the preceding chapters. Indeed my debt to these philosophers is much greater than the text may suggest, for the book is in large part an elaboration in a particular area of views they have espoused.

Other specific debts are less easily acknowledged, for they are unknown to or forgotten by the debtor. Any philosophical discussion is a co-operative enterprise, which leaves the participants enriched by new ideas of indeterminate authorship. Inevitably, therefore, some of this book will be derivative, but how much and from whom is impossible to say.

Besides such specific debts one has more general obligations. The perspective in which one sees philosophical problems, and the way in which one tries to solve them, are not innate but learnt. During my research I had the good fortune to be supervised by J. F. Bennett and M. K. Tanner in Cambridge, H. P. Grice and D. F. Pears in Oxford. I would like to take this opportunity to thank them, not only for the general influence they had upon my thought, but also for the trouble they took to read my work, and the benefit I derived from their criticism.

My examination, by B. A. O. Williams and R. Wollheim, was

a pleasant occasion whose details have unhappily slipped over the far edge of my memory span. Although I recall that they produced cogent objections to several points in my thesis, I cannot now remember what these were. It should not be thought, therefore, that the deficiencies in this book escaped unnoticed by my examiners.

In acknowledging a final debt I hope to remedy a possible injustice. My discussion of emotions and their objects springs from a critique of A. Kenny's *Action, Emotion, and Will.* Kenny's book brought many interesting questions into the philosophical arena. He presented clearly a point of view which is often presented confusedly, and in opposition to which I have tried to define my own position. It was through thinking about the questions he raised, and through attempting to articulate my dissatisfaction with his method of approach, that I arrived at my own views. As a result, my treatment of his book is rather critical, and is less than fair to its real merits. Without it, mine would not have been written.

Edinburgh, June 1971   J.R.S.W.

I

Introduction

Man has always accorded a special status to his kind. He has seen himself as distinct from the world around him. This intuitive conviction of his own uniqueness is reflected in his philosophy. But although philosophers – with the possible exception of Spinoza – agree that man is a special kind of thing, they differ in their account of what makes him special.

If one were giving a comprehensive account of the nature of a thing, one would have to describe it both from a static and from a dynamic point of view. That is, one would have, first, to say what it was made of and what it could be like, of what kind of elements it was composed and what kind of state it could be in at any particular time. One would also have, secondly, to give the principles according to which it changed its state, to say what laws governed its alterations and its interactions with other things. Correspondingly there are two ways in which things can differ radically in kind. There is a static difference of kind between two things if they differ radically in the elements of which they are composed, or the states which they can instantiate. There is a dynamic difference of kind between two things if they differ radically in the laws which govern their alterations and their interactions with other things.

Two accounts of the difference between man and the things which surround him are of particular importance for contemporary philosophy. Each sees the difference as a difference of kind, not just as a difference of degree of complexity of organisation, but whereas the first sees it as a static difference, the second sees it as a dynamic difference. The first, which has predominated for the last 300 years, is normally termed the Cartesian view. On this view, what marks off man from the inanimate objects around him is – varying with the particular version of the view in question – a matter of the elements of which he is composed, or the states which he can instantiate. As well as a body, in various physical states, he has a mind, or at least mental states. Thus far the Cartesian view is in agreement with the probable view of pre-philosophical man, who would take the difference between himself and an inanimate object to consist in his consciousness: he is aware, thinks, and acts, whereas sticks and stones, tables and chairs, do not. But the Cartesian view does not just affirm the undeniable fact that men think and stones do not; it asserts furthermore that this is a fundamental difference of kind, that the mental is not a form of the physical, and is in no way reducible to the physical.

The Cartesian view has been attacked recently, in particular by Ryle and Wittgenstein and their followers. But the rejection of Cartesian dualism has not resulted in the assimilation of man to the world around him. A new account of man's distinctness is given, not in terms of the elements of which he is composed, but in terms of the laws which govern his behaviour and his interactions with other things. The behaviour and interactions of physical things are governed by causal laws, and are wholly explicable in causal terms. The neo-Wittgensteinians deny the universal applicability of causal notions and causal explanations to the human realm. The spirit of the movement is well expressed in the following quotation from Winch: 'I want to show that the notion of a human society involves a scheme of concepts which is logically incompatible with the kinds of explanation offered in the natural sciences.'[1]

It would be misleading to suggest that a comprehensive alternative account is presented of man, his behaviour, and his interaction with his environment. Anti-causalism takes a more piecemeal form: in particular areas causal analyses and causal explanations are rejected. Thus Winch is concerned with man in his social aspect, insisting that the kind of explanation appropriate to human society, and the concepts in terms of which it must be examined, are of a fundamentally different kind from those appropriate to the behaviour and interaction of physical things. Other philosophers are more concerned with individual human actions. They say that actions are properly explicable in terms of reasons and motives, and that such explanations are not a form of causal explanation, and are not reducible to causal explanation. Some say that although

---

[1] P. Winch, *The Idea of a Social Science* (London, 1958), p. 72.

bodily movements may be causally explicable, actions are not. Other philosophers are concerned with human reactions and responses to things and events, or, in a more specialised field, to works of art, and deny that these can be understood in causal terms. But throughout there is an insistence that man is to be understood, and his behaviour is to be explained, in terms fundamentally different from those appropriate to physical objects. Once again man's distinctness is emphasised, this time not from a static point of view, because his make-up is different in kind from that of a physical object, but from a dynamic point of view, because his behaviour and reactions are governed by different principles and to be understood in different terms.

Again, of course, it is undeniable that a man's behaviour is explicable in terms of reasons and motives, whereas a stone's behaviour is not, or that a man's response to a work of art is importantly different from the reaction of litmus to acid. But the neo-Wittgensteinians' claim is that there is involved here not just a difference of degree, but a radical difference of kind, that explanation in terms of reasons is not a form of, is not reducible to, and indeed is incompatible with causal explanation, and that a man's response to a work of art is not to be understood in causal terms, however complex and sophisticated the analysis.

I have spoken as though the world contained men on the one hand, physical objects such as sticks and stones on the other, with nothing in between. But of course there are animals, exhibiting behaviour of varying degrees of complexity. Which side of the line should they be placed? Descartes notoriously denied consciousness to animals, viewing them as complicated machines. The position of the neo-Wittgensteinians is not clear on this matter, though Winch at one point contrasts a dog's habitual action with a man's rule-obeying one. In general they tend to ignore animals.

These two views of the special nature of man have not normally been held together, although they are not inconsistent. The Cartesians seem to have looked on the relation between mental events, and between mental events and physical events, as a causal one. Indeed one point of criticism of the Cartesian view has been that it treated explanation of behaviour in terms of a motive or a desire, for example, as explanation in terms of a prior, 'ghostly', mental event which caused the behaviour in question. Criticism of the view that a motive or desire is a mental event has not been distinguished from criticism of the view that explanation in terms of motives or desires is a form of causal explanation.

Recently, however, a reaction against anti-causalism has set in. More sophisticated causal views have been presented, notably by Davidson and Pears in articles to be mentioned later, which do not depend on Cartesian presumptions about the nature of the mind.[2] The present work can be viewed as belonging to this third, reactionary, stage.

2

To attack directly the very general issues raised in the previous section would be hopelessly ambitious. How the mental relates to the physical is the central problem in the philosophy of mind. This book will leave unsettled the question whether there is a fundamental static difference of kind between men and physical objects, as the Cartesians argue, or whether, as I am inclined to believe, some form of behaviourism or materialism is true. What I have to say about feelings such as emotions and sensations is compatible with either view, for behaviourists and materialists do not deny that people have feelings, but merely put forward a certain claim about how this is to be understood. Nor shall I attempt to show conclusively that all human activity falls under causal laws, and that explanation by reference to reasons is a form of causal explanation, although I believe that this is so, and although much of my discussion lends support to this thesis. I shall focus my attention on a more limited set of problems. These relate closely to the general themes introduced above, to which I shall return briefly in the concluding chapter.

The more limited problems on which I shall concentrate concern intentionality, a notion which is of particular relevance to both accounts of man's distinctness. It is of importance to the static account because certain philosophers have claimed that intentionality is the distinguishing mark of the mental. They have argued that mental phenomena are intentional and physical phenomena are not, and that therefore the mental cannot be a form of the physical.

[2] In a different area, that of perception, cf. also H. P. Grice, 'The Causal Theory of Perception', *Aristotelian Society Supplementary Volume*, xxxv (1961).

It is of importance to the dynamic account because certain philosophers, in particular Kenny, have denied that intentionality can be analysed in causal terms. As the arguments against a causal analysis of intentionality are very similar to those used in support of anti-causal positions elsewhere, an examination of their validity will be of general significance.

The notion of intentionality is normally introduced by saying that a phenomenon is intentional if it is directed to an object, or has a content. Thus mental states such as thoughts, desires and emotions are supposed all to be directed to objects, and it is this putative common feature which is called intentionality. Kenny largely limits his discussion to emotions and their objects, claiming that the emotion: object relation is not a causal one, and initially I shall follow suit. In Chapter vi I shall argue for a restricted use of the term 'object', such that some but not all intentional states have objects. Until then, the distinction is not important.

Kenny spells 'intentionality' as 'intensionality' throughout. This very easily leads to confusion. There are two distinct notions which may or may not have some connection with one another. What is normally spelt 'inten*t*ionality' is a supposed property of some or all mental states, roughly equivalent to 'being directed to an object'. Inten*s*ionality is opposed to extensionality, and is a property of sentences, or linguistic contexts. Attempts have been made to give criteria for the inten*t*ionality of mental states in terms of the inten*s*ionality of the sentences describing them, although I do not think that these have been successful. What Kenny has in mind is inten*t*ionality, i.e. a supposed property of mental states. Henceforth, to avoid confusion, I shall always spell this supposed property of mental states with a 't', amending quotations from Kenny accordingly.[3]

3

Whether or not causal notions are applicable to man's actions and reactions might seem to be a matter of empirical fact, and thus

[3] I have adopted what I think is majority usage, but other philosophers, for instance Chisholm and Anscombe, appear to diverge from this. It might be possible to settle the matter by reference to the history of the terms, but it does not seem to me particularly relevant to do so.

not the concern of philosophy. But the anti-causalists produce certain *a priori*, conceptual arguments in support of their position. Two of the most important of these are used by Kenny in his discussion of emotions and their objects. I attempt to show that these arguments are invalid, and thus that causal accounts cannot be ruled out in this *a priori* way. Although I consider these arguments in the particular context of the emotions, the objections I make are general ones.

If one wants to know whether a certain notion, or a certain kind of explanation, is a causal one, it is advisable first to look at the notion of cause. Discussions in the philosophy of mind are often vitiated by an over-simple idea of what counts as a causal explanation. I therefore preface the main discussion by briefly outlining an account of causation derived from Davidson.

The first anti-causal argument depends on the notion of a non-contingent connection. Kenny claims that an emotion is non-contingently connected to its object, and that consequently the relation between them cannot be a causal one. In Chapter III, I criticise the notion of a non-contingent connection in general. In Chapters IV and V, I examine Kenny's discussion in more detail.

The second argument takes as its starting-point certain facts about a person's knowledge of his own mind. It is claimed that the nature of this knowledge rules out a causal account of what is known. I discuss this argument in Chapters XII and XIII, and with it a variant of the dynamic account of man's distinctness, not previously mentioned, to the effect that although causal notions are applicable to man's thought and behaviour, the causation is of a particular 'mental' kind, not analysable in a Humean way. I try to show that the relevant facts about self-knowledge can be reconciled with the claim that a perfectly normal, Humean kind of causation is involved in the mental sphere.

What might appear to be a third anti-causal argument is mentioned in Chapter IX, 4. It may be felt that to see the emotion: object relation in causal terms is to rule out a certain kind of assessment or appraisal of the object, or of the response to the object. This is not in itself really an argument, for the kind of assessment or appraisal in question could quite well be in fact inappropriate. The feeling, however, may be one of the motives behind anti-causalism, and I try to show that it is unfounded.

In Chapters VI to XI I discuss emotions and their objects in a more positive way. I restrict the term 'object' to items existing in the world, and attempt to outline the conditions under which an emotion has a particular item as its object. I suggest that the relation of an emotion to its object is indeed causal. In Chapter xiv I attempt to meet a possible objection to my account, to the effect that it fails to answer the important questions. In Chapter xv I discuss what I treat as the more general notion of intentionality. I argue that this is in fact a viable notion, that many mental states do share an important feature which can be explained in terms of content, but that it is an illusion to suppose that appeal to intentionality provides an easy way of showing that the mental is not a form of the physical.

In the last part of the book I plunge into what could more properly be called philosophical logic or philosophy of language. Contemporary Anglo-Saxon philosophy is often called linguistic, but what exactly this means is not always clear. No doubt philosophy is concerned with the concepts we use to think about the world, and this is in some complex way a matter of the language we use to talk about the world. But some discussions in philosophy of mind, particularly discussions of intentionality, are linguistic in a much more straightforward sense than this. They give an account of intentionality directly in terms of logico-grammatical features of the statements used to report intentional states. I argue in Chapter vii that this kind of approach is unsatisfactory, for it proceeds in quite the wrong direction. An account of intentionality has to be given at a substantive level. If reports of intentional states must possess certain logico-grammatical features, this is to be explained by reference to the phenomena reported. The statements used to report intentional states undoubtedly do raise questions of interpretation. I discuss these in Chapters xvi to xviii, and attempt to show that they can be illuminatingly related to substantive issues in the philosophy of mind.

II

Causal relations

I

Items in the world – people, objects, events, states of affairs, etc. –
may bear different relations to one another. Thus any two people
may be related as father to son, as master to slave, as lawyer to
client, as teacher to student, or in many other ways. Relations are
often the object of philosophical analysis. Part of our concern is with
the nature of a relation, the emotion: object relation. We want to
know what this relation consists in. That is, we want to know what
it is for two items in the world to be related as emotion to object.
In particular, we want to know whether this relation can properly
be said to be a causal one. Not all relations are causal ones. For
example, spatial and temporal relations, and relations of similarity
and difference, are not. Is it a necessary condition for two items
to be related as emotion to object that a certain kind of causal relation exist between them? Or is it the case, as Kenny claims,
that the emotion: object relation cannot be analysed in causal terms?

As the notion of cause is so central to my concern, I ought to
begin by discussing it. In this chapter I shall give a brief account
which is based on an article by Davidson.[1] Davidson talks about
one causal relation in particular, the cause: effect relation, but I
shall suggest that other relations besides this can properly be called
causal, and that there are forms of causal explanations of events
which do not consist in citing a cause.

I believe that this preliminary discussion of causation is worth-
while. As I said in Chapter 1, many recent writers in the philosophy of mind have advanced anti-causal theses, particularly with
regard to the relation between the mind and behaviour. For example, they have tried to show that explanation of behaviour in
terms of desires, motives, emotions, etc., is not a form of causal

[1] D. Davidson, 'Causal Relations', *Journal of Philosophy*, LXIV (1967).
See also D. Davidson, 'Actions, Reasons and Causes', *Journal of
Philosophy*, LX (1963).

explanation. Defects in their discussions can often be traced to an unduly restricted idea of what counts as a causal explanation. Thus some philosophers have thought that to show that explanation in terms of motives is not a form of causal explanation, it is sufficient to show that a motive is not a cause. In Section 3 of this chapter I suggest briefly how philosophers may have been misled by an inadequate notion of cause.

2

Davidson is concerned not with the analysis of causation – with whether it can be analysed in terms of constant conjunction, for example – but with the logical form of singular causal statements. He claims that contemporary attempts to show that 'caused' is a disguised sentential connective are misguided. Instead singular causal statements report a relation between particular events. Strictly speaking, therefore, the cause of one event is always another event. If one event causes another, they must be covered by a causal law, which Davidson tentatively suggests might have the form of a conjunction: If event u causes event v then there must be properties F and G such that Fu and Gv and some law (L) holds to the effect that whenever an F event occurs, it causes a G event which occurs epsilon later, and whenever a G event occurs, it is caused by an F event which occurs epsilon earlier. Put symbolically:

$$(x)(n)((Fx \ \& \ t_x=n) \rightarrow (\exists!y)(Gy \ \& \ t_y=n+\epsilon \ \& \ Cxy))$$
(L) and
$$(x)(n)((Gx \ \& \ t_x=n+\epsilon) \rightarrow (\exists!y)Fy \ \& \ t_y=n \ \& \ Cyx))$$

'x' and 'y' range over events, 'n' ranges over numbers, F and G are properties of events, 'Cxy' is read 'x causes y', and 't' is a function that assigns a number to an event to mark the time the event occurs. From this law, together with a premiss to the effect that an event of a certain description exists:

$$(P) \qquad\qquad (\exists!x)(Fx \ \& \ t_x=3),$$

we could infer a singular causal statement saying that the event caused another:

$(C) \qquad (\imath x)(Fx \ \& \ t_x=3)$ caused $(\imath x)(Gx \ \& \ t_x=3+\epsilon).^2$

The precise details of this do not matter. The important thing is

---

[2] Cf. Davidson, 'Causal Relations', pp. 699ff. I have slightly altered Davidson's presentation.

that if one event causes another, there must be descriptions of these events which figure in a true causal law.

Just as the same object can be described or referred to in different ways, so the same event can be referred to or reported in different ways. Thus I might report the same event by saying 'Smith struck a match at 3 o'clock', or 'Smith struck a match in a gas-filled room at 3 o'clock', or even 'An event occurred at 3 o'clock which caused an explosion'. Causal statements are extensional. That is, if some statement truly says that one event caused another, any statement derived from this by substituting another description of one of the events referred to will also be true. Conversely a causal statement can be true even if it refers to cause and effect by means of descriptions which cannot be generalised over, i.e. such that no causal law covers all events answering to just those descriptions.

This is important, for it shows that one can hold a Humean view of causation while admitting that no singular causal statement entails any particular causal law. All that a singular causal statement entails is that there is some causal law covering the events in question. Again,

Mill ... was wrong in thinking we have not specified the whole cause of an event when we have not wholly specified it. And there is not, as Mill and others have maintained, anything elliptical in the claim that a certain man's death was caused by his eating a particular dish, even though death resulted only because the man had a particular bodily constitution, a particular state of present health, and so on.[3]

As regards our evidence for singular causal statements, Davidson says that

The great majority of singular causal statements are not backed, we may be sure, by laws in the way (C) is backed by (L). The relation in general is rather this: if 'a caused b' is true, then there are descriptions of a and b such that the result of substituting them for 'a' and 'b' in 'a caused b' is entailed by true premisses of the form of (L) and (P); and the converse holds if suitable restrictions are put on the descriptions. If this is correct, it does not follow that we must be able to dredge up a law if we know a singular causal statement to be true; all that follows is that we know there must be a covering law. And very often, I think, our justification for accepting a singular causal statement is that we have reason to believe an appropriate causal law exists, though we do not know what it is.[4]

[3] *Ibid*. p. 698.   [4] *Ibid*. p. 701.

Our ground for thinking that some causal law does cover a given case, and hence for thinking that a particular singular causal statement is true, is often knowledge of some generalisation that normally holds – not necessarily a causal law, or even a first approximation to one.

Generalisations like 'If you strike a well-made match hard enough against a properly prepared surface, then, other conditions being favourable, it will light' owe their importance not to the fact that we can hope eventually to render them untendentious and exceptionless, but rather to the fact that they summarise much of our evidence for believing that full-fledged causal laws exist covering events we wish to explain.[5]

The causal law covering the case would probably be quantitative, and might employ completely different concepts to the generalisation which provides evidence for its existence.[6]

This is Davidson's account of the central cause: effect relation. The case he makes out for it in his article seems entirely adequate, so I shall not attempt to argue for it here. However, I think that there are other relations derived from the central cause : effect relation which can also properly be called causal.

If one event causes another, some description of that event will figure in the relevant causal law. Let us call this the generalisable description. The generalisable description may refer to the circumstances in which the cause occurred, or to some state of affairs which obtained at that time. Thus if Smith's striking a match caused an explosion, the generalisable description may have to mention the presence of gas in the room. In such a case we can say that the state of affairs in question and the effect – the presence of gas in the room and the explosion – are causally related, even though they are not strictly speaking related as cause to effect. This relation might be called the relation of causally relevant factor to effect.

Again, sometimes a cause is an event involving a certain person or thing. In the example given above, the cause is Smith's striking a match. Here also we can say that the person or thing in question and the effect – Smith and the explosion – are causally related, although they are not related as cause to effect. This relation might be called the relation of agent to effect.

Other relations derived from the central cause: effect relation can be called causal. For example, there is the relation of agent to thing

---

[5] *Ibid.*   [6] Cf. Davidson, 'Actions, Reasons and Causes', p. 697.

acted upon. Again, if one event figures in the causal history of another event, but they are not sufficiently close in time to be called
cause and effect, they are nonetheless causally related. Further examples could be given, but enough has been said to show that there
is a cluster of relations centring around the cause: effect relation
which can all properly be called causal. Now when we say that a
relation like the stimulus: response relation or the emotion: object
relation is causal, we mean that it is a necessary condition for two
items to be related as stimulus to response, or as emotion to object,
that they be causally related in one of the possible ways. The notion
of cause must enter into the analysis of the relation in question.
Thus the stimulus: response relation is a causal one, since part of
what is involved in something being a response to a stimulus
is that it be caused by the stimulus.

To say that a certain relation is causal is to say that for two
items to be related in that way, the causal network in which they are
enmeshed must conform to a certain pattern. It leaves open the
possibility that the particular way in which the pattern is instantiated may be different in different cases. Thus the relation of murderer to victim is a causal one. To say that one man is the murderer
of another is to say that the first played a certain kind of causal
role in the death of the second. But how he played this role – what
the particular causal story was, and what causal laws covered the
murder – may vary from case to case. There may not be any causal
laws covering all murders. Indeed it may not be particularly useful
to look for causal laws in trying to understand murders.[7]

In this way, if the emotion: object relation is a causal one, it
doesn't follow that the same kind of object always elicits the same
kind of emotion. Nor, if the same object elicits a similar emotion
in two different people, does it follow that the underlying causal
story is the same in each case. Furthermore there is no implication that talk of objects is superfluous, or that it could be replaced
without loss by talk of causes. Similarly if the concept of a reason
for action is a causal concept, it doesn't follow that it can be dis-

[7] This is of obvious relevance to the social sciences. Even if all human
action is covered by causal laws, it does not follow that social scientists
should look for such causal laws. They may only exist at the neuro-
physiological level. Understanding a social phenomenon is certainly
not to be equated with bringing it under an exceptionless generalisation.

pensed with, or that explanation in terms of reasons is not a form of explanation peculiar to the behaviour of conscious beings.

Just as there are various causal relations, so there are various types of explanation which can be called causal. One way of causally explaining an event is to say what its cause was. But one can causally explain an event without mentioning its cause at all, perhaps by referring to a causally relevant factor. What counts as explanatory for a particular person depends in part upon what he already knows and why he wants an explanation in the first place. Even if one does explain by mentioning the cause, it may be more explanatory or informative to refer to it by one description than by another. I shall not go into the details of this, but shall suggest merely that a description may be more informative as it brings the cause more into line with whatever generalisation covers the case. Thus the occurrence of an explosion is more satisfactorily explained by 'Someone struck a match in a room full of gas' than by 'Someone struck a match', because it is more nearly true that striking a match in a room full of gas always causes an explosion than that striking a match always causes an explosion. In some cases one can satisfactorily explain an event simply by mentioning the circumstances in which the cause occurred, either because the cause is already known, or because, given that the circumstances were of that kind, it is obvious what kind of event the cause must have been. Here, even though one has explained the event without mentioning the cause, the explanation is still a causal one.

Sometimes we explain an event by reference to the presence of a disposition: a piece of glass broke because it was brittle, one piece of iron attracted another because it was magnetised. I think that this is also a form of causal explanation, for explanation by reference to a dispositional property is only satisfactory if this dispositional property is itself causally explicable in terms of underlying structural properties (although I don't want to imply that we must know what these underlying structural properties are). I shall not attempt to argue this here.

It is of course true that in everyday speech we refer to items other than events as causes, and Davidson admits that this is so. Sometimes we refer to a causally relevant state of affairs as a cause: 'The cause of the explosion was the presence of gas in the room'. Sometimes we even speak of a physical object or person as a cause: 'Smith is the cause of all my troubles', 'The wire caused him to trip over'. Such sentences can normally be spelt out in terms of causal relations between events – what caused the troubles, or the tripping over, was some event or events concerning Smith, or the wire. Sometimes we seem to cite a fact, rather than an event, as a cause. Davidson gives examples, such as 'The failure of the sprinkling system caused the fire', or 'The collapse was caused, not by the fact that the bolt gave way, but by the fact that it gave way so suddenly and unexpectedly'. He says that

Some of these sentences may yield to the methods I have prescribed, especially if failures are counted among events, but others remain recalcitrant. What we must say in such cases is that in addition to, or in place of, giving what Mill calls the 'producing cause', such sentences tell, or suggest, a causal story. They are, in other words, rudimentary causal explanations. Explanations typically relate statements, not events. I suggest therefore that the 'caused' of the sample sentences in this paragraph is not the 'caused' of straightforward singular causal statements, but is best expressed by the words 'causally explains'.[8]

Apart from the exceptions mentioned, most of our everyday causal talk seems to accord with Davidson's account, and the exceptions seem to diverge in explicable ways. I shall therefore assume that his account is essentially correct, and shall operate in terms of it henceforward.

3

I suggested earlier that some discussions in the philosophy of mind suffer through an over-simple notion of cause. I shall briefly outline two ways in which this may happen.

(1) Some philosophers seem to have thought that if a statement is causal, it must have been arrived at by induction from similar instances, and that since certain statements, in particular statements about one's own mind, are clearly not arrived at in this way, they cannot be causal. Two points can be made about this. First, it should be clear from the preceding discussion that one can have grounds for asserting a singular causal statement even if one does not know what the relevant causal law is. A singular causal statement implies only that some causal law covers the case. One can

[8] Davidson, 'Causal Relations', p. 703.

have grounds for thinking that this is so even when one does not know what the causal law in question is, and one's grounds need not be based on the consideration of similar instances. Secondly, a statement can be causal even if it is not based on the consideration of evidence at all. To say that a statement is causal is not to say that it is based on a certain kind of evidence, but rather that it is answerable to and corrigible in the light of a certain kind of evidence. I shall return to this point later.

(2) Some philosophers have thought that to show that a motive or a desire is not a cause (perhaps because it is not an 'internal impression' or an 'inner event') is *ipso facto* to show that explanation in terms of motives or desires is not a form of causal explanation. This assumption runs through Melden's *Free Action*, and occurs to a lesser extent in other books in the same series.[9] It is even accepted by Ryle, who says that an argument

takes it for granted that to explain an act as done from a certain motive, in this case from vanity, is to give a causal explanation. This means that it assumes that a mind, in this case the boaster's mind, is a field of special causes.[10]

This assumption is mistaken. As we have seen, a type of explanation can properly be called causal even if it is not explanation by reference to a cause. And to say that explanation in terms of motives or desires is a form of causal explanation does not commit one to the view that motives or desires are events. Perhaps desires admit of a dispositional analysis. If so, explanation in terms of desires is a form of dispositional explanation, and thus, if my claim is correct, a form of causal explanation. Furthermore, if beliefs, desires, etc., admit of a dispositional analysis, there would be no conflict between an explanation of someone's behaviour in terms of his beliefs and desires, and an explanation of his behaviour in terms of antecedent causes, any more than there is a conflict between a dispositional explanation of the behaviour of a physical object and an explanation of that behaviour in terms of antecedent causes.

[9] A. I. Melden, *Free Action* (London, 1961), in the series 'Studies in Philosophical Psychology', edited by R. F. Holland.
[10] G. Ryle, *The Concept of Mind* (London, 1948), p. 86.

4

If Davidson's account is correct, only events can be causes. The everyday notion of the object of an emotion is a somewhat imprecise one, but certainly items other than events – people and physical objects, for example – are commonly referred to as objects of emotions. Hence many objects of emotion are simply of the wrong category to be causes.

A causal theorist of any sophistication would not, therefore, just equate the object of an emotion with its cause, or claim that the emotion: object relation was the effect: cause relation. He would claim rather that the emotion: object relation was to be analysed in causal terms. Thus he might claim that an item is the object of an emotion if and only if the item figures in the causal history of the emotion in an appropriate way. What the appropriate way was might depend on the emotion and the type of object in question, but in any case it would be by virtue of the way an item figured in the causal history of an emotion that it qualified as the object of that emotion.

Unfortunately Kenny, with whose anti-causal arguments I shall be concerned, seems to use the word 'cause' rather casually. He argues that the relation of emotion to object is not that of effect to cause, and that in general the objects of emotions must be distinguished from their causes. His use of 'cause' does not correspond to Davidson's, for he refers to items other than events as causes. Yet he cannot be taken to mean by 'cause' any causally relevant factor, since he seems to assume that in any case there is just one item to be picked out as *the* cause. Consider, for instance, the following passage:

For both [Descartes and Hume], to say that a child is afraid of the fire is to say that the mental event which is his fear is the effect of which the fire he now sees is the cause... When the burnt child dreads the fire, the object of his fear is the fire which is here and now afraid of; but his present fear is the effect of his past experience.[11]

Would it not be most natural to say that both the child's past experience and his present experience are causally relevant to his fear? Here and throughout his discussion Kenny seems to operate with an

[11] A. Kenny, *Action, Emotion, and Will (AEW)* (London, 1963), p. 71.

over-simple notion of cause.[12] But his arguments will be of most interest if we take him to be opposing not just the naive theory (which surely no philosopher can have held) that the object of an emotion is always its cause, but also any more sophisticated causal theory.

[12] This may be partly derived from Wittgenstein. Between the two sentences quoted above, Kenny quotes from L. Wittgenstein, *Philosophical Investigations* (Oxford, 1953), Part 1, §476. Cf. also L. Wittgenstein, *Zettel* (Oxford, 1967), §488.

III

Non-contingent relations

I

Before I attempt to give a substantive account of the emotion: object relation, I wish first to consider a general argument which, if valid, would show that it cannot be analysed in causal terms. This argument claims that the relation, or connection (these terms are normally used interchangeably) of an emotion to its object is a non-contingent (i.e. necessary) one, and hence that it cannot be a causal one. It has been advanced most notably by Kenny. As I said at the end of the last chapter, Kenny has an over-simple notion of cause, and the objection, to be interesting, must be taken as directed against any causal theory.

Kenny's claim that an emotion is non-contingently connected to its object is one of a family of similar claims. He himself also argues that an emotion is non-contingently connected to its manifestation in behaviour, and hence that this relation cannot be a causal one either. Other philosophers of the same school have advanced similar arguments, hoping thereby to justify a sharp distinction between explanation in terms of reasons and motives, and causal explanation.[1]

Many of the arguments adduced to show that explanation in terms of reasons is not a form of causal explanation have been competently criticised by Davidson and Pears.[2] However, they do not discuss in great detail the general notion of a non-contingent connection. Thus although my discussion will be addressed particu-

---

[1] Such arguments occur in several books in the previously-mentioned series, 'Studies in Philosophical Psychology', especially in Melden's *Free Action*. See also, for example, C. Taylor, *The Explanation of Behaviour* (London, 1964).

[2] Davidson in 'Actions, Reasons and Causes', D. F. Pears in 'Are Reasons for Actions Causes?', in A. Stroll (ed.), *Epistemology* (New York, 1967), and in 'Desires as Causes of Actions', in *The Human Agent, Royal Institute of Philosophy Lectures*, Vol. 1 (London, 1968).

larly to the emotion: object case, it will have a wider relevance. There are certain important differences, nevertheless, between the argument from non-contingency as applied to the emotion: object relation, and as applied to the mental state: manifestation in behaviour relation. In brief, in the latter case the non-contingent connection is supposed to relate two states or modifications of one item, for example someone's wanting something and his behaving in a certain way; in the former case it is generally supposed to relate two clearly distinct items, for example someone's fear and a dog.[3]

In this chapter I will discuss generally the notion of a non-contingent connection, deferring until Chapters IV and V a consideration of Kenny's particular use of it. I will try to show that if a non-contingent connection is taken to be a certain kind of connection, as seems to be intended, then the very idea is an illegitimate one. The claim that a relation is a causal one is a claim about the nature or analysis of the relation itself. If there were to be any opposition between causality, and necessity or non-contingency, some sense would have to attach to the notion of a necessary or non-contingent connection as a certain kind of connection. I will argue, however, that only propositions, facts, etc., can properly be said to be necessary or contingent, and that even if it is necessary *that* an item of one type should have a certain connection or relation to an item of another type, this does not license the inference to the necessity or non-contingency of the connection or relation itself.

2

With certain qualifications which I shall consider later, emotions and their objects are particular items in the world. The emotion: object relation thus relates particular items in the world. Our aim is to discover when this relation holds between two items in the world, i.e. under what conditions two items will be related in this way. We must note that any two items will always be related in some way, even if only temporally. Furthermore even if two items are related as X to Y, they may be related in other ways as well. Two people may be related as father to son, and also, for instance, be like one another. Similarly an emotion and its object may be related in ways other than as emotion to object – for instance, if I am

[3] See Section 4, below.

ashamed of what I have done, the object of my emotion is prior to my emotion. We are concerned, of course, to examine the emotion: object relation, and not any other relation which may happen to hold between an emotion and its object.

If the emotion: object relation relates particular items, then if the emotion: object relation is a non-contingent relation, at least some non-contingent relations must relate particular items. But we need to know in more detail how the notion of a non-contingent relation is supposed to work. What exactly is being said of a relation when it is said to be non-contingent? There seem *prima facie* to be two possibilities.

(1) If we say that a relation is a causal relation, we are making a substantive claim about the nature of the relation. We are saying that it can be analysed in causal terms. One possibility is that the claim that a relation is a non-contingent relation is intended as a similarly substantive claim about the nature of the relation. That is, perhaps such a claim about a relation is to be thought of as an analysis, or the first step towards an analysis, of the relation.

(2) The second possibility is that relations are supposed to fall into two general categories. To say that a relation is contingent or non-contingent would not be to make a substantive claim about the nature or analysis of the relation, but simply to allot it to one or other of these two categories. If all causal relations are contingent ones, and if the emotion: object relation is a non-contingent one, it would follow that the emotion: object relation couldn't be a kind of causal relation. But saying that it was a non-contingent relation would not be saying *what* relation it was, any more than saying that a relation was a contingent relation would be saying what relation it was. There would be different kinds of contingent relations – causal relations, relations of similarity, temporal relations, and so on – and similarly, on this alternative, there would be different kinds of non-contingent relations. If this were how the notion was to be understood, then in saying that the emotion: object relation is non-contingent, one would not be offering an analysis of that relation. One would not be putting forward a proper alternative to a causal theory, but would merely be showing that any causal theory must be incorrect. The substantive positive job would remain to be done.

When Kenny says that a relation is non-contingent, it is not clear which way his claim is to be taken. Normally his argument is that the emotion: object relation is a non-contingent one, that all causal connections are contingent ones, and that therefore the emotion: object relation is not a causal one. However, he seems to think that it is sufficient to say that the emotion: object relation is a non-contingent one. At least, having shown, as he thinks, that the relation is not a causal one, he doesn't then go on to outline any theory which could serve as a proper alternative to a causal theory. This suggests that he thinks that in showing that the emotion: object relation is a non-contingent one, he has done enough – that he has thereby given a substantive account of the relation.

3

I want now to suggest that no sense attaches to the claim that a connection or relation is contingent or non-contingent, unless this is understood as meaning that it is contingent or non-contingent *that* there is a connection or relation of a certain kind between certain items. Furthermore, if the claim is understood in this way, then it cannot be used in support of any anti-causal claim. The necessary/contingent contrast has its primary application in the context of talk about statements, propositions, facts, truths, etc. (I do not wish to discuss the relation between these, or which has priority.) A necessary proposition is one that can be shown to be true without reference to the facts – it is necessarily true, true *a priori*. A contingent proposition is one whose truth or falsity can only be determined by reference to the facts – it is contingently true, true *a posteriori*. Thus we say that it is a necessary proposition, or necessarily true, that if anything is a brother, it is male, whereas it is a contingent proposition, or contingently true (or false), that if anything is a brother, it is irascible. Most philosophers would now accept that propositions can be shown to be true without reference to the facts if and only if they can be shown to be true by means of conceptual analysis.

A necessary *proposition* is one that is necessarily *true*. But a *relation* cannot be true or false any more than a property can, so it cannot be necessarily or contingently true or false. Of course it can be true that a certain item has a certain property, or that a certain relation holds between two items. It can be necessarily true that if something has one property or belongs to one kind, then it has another property or belongs to another kind. Thus it is necessarily true that if something is a father, then it is male. Similarly it can be necessarily true that if something is of one kind, then there is something of another kind to which it is related in a certain way. Thus it is necessarily true that if someone is a father, then there is some person to whom he is related as parent to child. But saying this does not tell us anything about the nature of the relation in question.

Someone might think that he had established something about the nature of a relation or connection if without noticing he made the following series of moves:

1 necessarily (or non-contingently) any *A* is related (or connected) to a *B*.

2 therefore any *A* is, necessarily, related to a *B*.

3 therefore any *A* is necessarily-related to a *B*.

1 clearly tells us nothing about the nature of the *A*:*B* relation. But it would be possible to move from 1 to 3, which seems to say that the *A*:*B* relation is of a certain kind, namely that it is a necessary or non-contingent relation, and from this to conclude that therefore it cannot be a causal relation.

This is obviously invalid. Even if necessarily any father is related to some child, nothing follows about the nature of the father: child relation, and in particular it does not follow that it is not a causal relation. Again, it is true that necessarily any cause is connected to some effect. If the argument were valid, it would follow that any cause is necessarily-connected to some effect, and hence that it couldn't be causally connected to that effect. This is clearly absurd.[4] I cannot prove that all philosophers who have talked of relations or connections as necessary or non-contingent have arrived at this conclusion by way of an illicit move of the kind suggested, but it seems to me the most probable route. In Chapter v I shall argue that Kenny has certainly followed it.

[4] In this latter connection, compare Kant's possible conflation of the thesis that causal laws are necessary, meaning that there must be causal laws, with the thesis that causal laws are necessary, meaning that causal laws express some non-empirical kind of necessity. This seems to be precisely the same kind of illicit move from a point about scope or application to a point about analysis. Cf. J. F. Bennett, *Kant's Analytic* (Cambridge, England, 1966), p. 155.

Generally there is no reason why things shouldn't be classified into kinds on a wholly or partly causal basis. If the basis of classifying things as Ks is causal, then it will be necessary that if something is a K, it has a certain causal relation to something else. Clearly the fact that this is a necessary truth cannot cast any aspersions on the claim of the relation in question to be causal. If two kinds $K1$ and $K2$ are such that necessarily anything belonging to $K1$ has relation R to some member of $K2$, one might call R a necessary relation, but the only purpose this seems to serve is to mislead.

It is worth saying slightly more on the subject of necessary propositions about relations or connections. The examples given have been hypothetical – they have been of the form: 'If something is an A, then . . .' But some propositions assert a relation or connection between two particular items. It might be claimed that if such a categorical proposition were necessary, this would legitimise talk of the relation or connection itself as necessary. In reply to this, two points can be made.

(1) A statement asserting a connection between two particular items should surely be extensional. That is, the *truth* of such a statement should not depend on the particular descriptions employed to refer to the items in question. But the modal value of a statement does depend on the particular descriptions employed. That is, if any statement asserting a connection between two items was necessary, this would be by virtue of the particular descriptions chosen to describe those items, and it would always be possible to substitute some other description of one of the items which would render the statement contingent.

(2) But in any case no statement asserting that a particular item has a property, or that two particular items are related in a certain way, can be necessarily true, whatever descriptions are chosen. Any such statement will always entail a contingent statement, and no necessary statement can entail a contingent one. For this reason Davidson is conceding too much when he says:

Suppose 'A caused B' is true. Then the cause of $B = A$; so, substituting, we have 'The cause of B caused B', which is analytic. The truth of a causal statement depends on *what* events are described; its status as analytic or synthetic depends on *how* the events are described.[5]

He is surely wrong, for 'The cause of B caused B' entails such

[5] Davidson, 'Actions, Reasons and Causes', p. 234.

contingent propositions as that *B* exists, that the cause of *B* exists, that something caused *B*, and so on, and therefore cannot itself be necessary.[6]

To sum up, I wish to assert: first, that modal values can be attached only to facts, propositions, and the like, and not to properties or relations; secondly, that from the necessity of a proposition or fact, no anti-causal conclusion can be drawn. Note that in opposing Kenny and those philosophers who take a similar line, I do not say that an emotion is only contingently related to its object, or that a sensation is only contingently related to its manifestation in behaviour. Such a claim is no more legitimate than its contrary, for a relation can be neither necessary nor contingent. Similarly I think that Kenny is wrong to say that causal connections are contingent.[7] It is contingent that one event causes another. It is necessary that if a wound is fatal, it causes death. Neither of these propositions licenses the move to saying that the causal connection itself is necessary or contingent.

4

Behind the illegitimate talk of non-contingent connections may lie a valid anti-causal argument which has been unfortunately expressed. In this section I shall examine what seems to me to be the most likely line of argument.

On one occasion Kenny talks not of a non-contingent connection, but of a conceptual connection: 'There is a conceptual connection also between a feeling and its object, whereas the physiological processes studied by psychologists lack intentionality.'[8] Elsewhere he says that certain connections are not contingent, since a man who was unaware of them would not possess the concept of the emotions in question.[9] When someone says that there is a conceptual connection between an *A* and a *B*, or between *A*s and *B*s, he may mean that there is a connection between the concept of an *A* and the concept of a *B*. The argument would then take this form:

---

[6] Some might wish to say, wrongly in my opinion, that a statement presupposes, rather than entails, the existence of the things referred to. This would not affect my point, for the last entailment suggested would still hold.

[7] Kenny, *AEW*, pp. 14, 24, 26.　　　[8] *Ibid*. p. 38.　　　[9] *Ibid*. p. 100.

if there is a certain kind of connection between the concept of an
A and the concept of a *B*, *A*s cannot be causally connected to *B*s.
Perhaps we could restate Kenny's references to non-contingent con-
nections in this way.

I agree that there are conceptual connections, if this is understood
to mean connections between concepts. Such conceptual connections
or relations may be of various kinds. Sometimes two concepts are
related in that any item which falls under one falls under the
other. Thus anything falling under the concept father falls under
the concept male. Sometimes two concepts are related in that any
item which falls under one has a certain relation to some item falling under the other. Thus any item falling under the concept father
has a certain relation to some item falling under the concept child;
any item falling under the concept cause has a certain relation to
some item falling under the concept effect. In some such cases it
may be true that someone who did not know of this relation would
not possess the concepts in question. Thus someone who was unaware of the cause: effect relation would not have the concept of
a cause. It can be necessary that two concepts are related in a certain way – for instance it is necessary that anything falling under
the concept father falls under the concept male. But it is of course
no more legitimate to speak of the relation between concepts as
contingent or necessary than it is so to speak of the relation between
particular items.

If the concept of an *A* and the concept of a *B* are related in that
any item falling under the first concept must bear a certain relation
to some item falling under the second, then one can establish on
conceptual grounds – i.e. without reference to the empirical facts –
that any *A* is connected to a *B*. Could this show that the *A:B*
relation is not a causal one? The argument sometimes takes the
following specific form: if it is possible to establish on conceptual
grounds that there is a connection between items of one type and
items of another type, then there cannot be a causal connection
between items of the types in question, since a causal connection is
one that can only be established inductively. Thus Kenny: 'The
relation between the passion and this idea is one of cause and effect,
and therefore, on Hume's general principles, a contingent one, inductively established.'[10] However, this won't do. What one can

[10] *Ibid.* p. 24.

establish on conceptual grounds is that *if* any item belongs to one type, say T_1, then it must have a certain relation, say R, to some item belonging to another type, say T_2. That is, it may be necessary that *if* x is of type T_1, then there is some y such that y is of type T_2 and xRy. But to establish that x *is* of type T_1 one must establish that there is some other item of type T_2, and that the relation between the two items is of the right kind, and to establish *this* may be a matter of induction.

The argument is sometimes modified as follows: if two items are causally related, then it must be possible in some sense to describe or identify either item without making use of the fact that it is related to the other. Thus Kenny says of a suggestion of Ryle's:

Now if this cause-effect story is to be the true one, it must be possible to identify the effect independently of the cause. We must be able to say 'This is the same kind of twinge as I felt yesterday', without making any appeal to what the twinge is a twinge *of* as a criterion of identity.[11]

Similarly Melden:

Now in general if A causes B, a description of A other than that it has the causal property of producing B must be forthcoming . . .[12]

If the relation were causal, the wanting to do would be, indeed it must be describable independently of any reference to the doing.[13]

Even Pears, who criticises these philosophers, operates in terms of a principle of this kind, though it is not clear if he himself accepts it.

Suppose that we say that A cannot cause B unless A can be specified in some way that does not mention the fact that it causes B.[14]

A cause . . . must be identifiable under a description which does not connect it causally with its supposed effect.[15]

There does seem to be something to this argument, as can be seen by referring back to the account of causal statements. If one event u causes another event v, then there must be descriptions of u and v which occur in a true causal law. But it seems to follow from a Humean account of causation that *these* descriptions must be such that it is not analytic that any event answering to the first description is followed by an event answering to the second description.

[11] *Ibid.* p. 80.   [12] *Free Action*, p. 46.   [13] *Ibid.* p. 128.
[14] 'Desires as Causes of Actions', p. 87.
[15] 'Are Reasons for Actions Causes?', p. 215.

However, if one could not give independent descriptions of the relevant kind of two events, this would surely cast doubt on the distinctness of the two events. If two items are genuinely distinct, and if they belong to the same ontological category (that is, if they are both events, or both physical objects, or whatever), then it must be logically possible that one should have existed and not the other. In this eventuality, there would have been some way of identifying or describing the one that did exist. This way, which *ex hypothesi* could not refer to the second item, must still be available if the second item exists.

This suggests that philosophers who speak of non-contingent connections might sometimes be able to reformulate their position. They may be trying to point out a genuine contrast between situations which can be described as consisting of two causally connected items, and situations which cannot be so described. But whereas they have represented this as a contrast between situations where two items are contingently connected and situations where two items are non-contingently connected, it should more properly be represented as a contrast between situations where two items are causally connected, and situations where there are not two distinct items at all. For example, someone who said that a desire or emotion was non-contingently connected to its manifestation in behaviour, and therefore could not cause it, might reformulate his position thus: a desire or emotion isn't something distinct from its manifestation in behaviour, and hence cannot be causally related to it, for relations only hold between distinct items.

I shall not consider this possibility any further, since fairly clearly it will not do in the case of emotion and object. If I am afraid of a dog, the dog and my fear are distinct items in any sense of the word. In the passages quoted earlier in this section, the point was sometimes put in terms of description, and sometimes of identification, but what was really at issue was the former. Kenny does have another argument which concerns identification proper, and which I shall consider in Chapter v.

IV

Kenny's aims

In the last chapter I gave general reasons for rejecting the notion of a non-contingent connection. In this chapter and the next I shall consider Kenny's particular discussion of the emotion: object relation. There are several reasons why this merits quite detailed attention.

(1) The general accusations which I made in the last chapter demand substantiation. I suggested that philosophers have come to talk of non-contingent connections by a rather obviously illicit route. I shall try to support my claim that this is in fact how they arrive at the notion by a close examination of Kenny's arguments.

(2) One of Kenny's aims is to show that the emotion: object relation is not causal, but this by no means exhausts the interest of what he says. He raises and discusses a number of different issues in the course of his very wide-ranging book, and some of these are relevant to our topic. Even if his talk of non-contingent connections is to be rejected, this does not in itself invalidate the rest of his discussion.

(3) One of Kenny's main purposes is to show that the traditional theories of the emotions held by such philosophers as Descartes and Hume were misconceived. Many modern writers have attacked the Cartesian theory of the mind, but I think that often the criticism has been unfair, that there is a general tendency to attribute to the traditional philosophers theories less tenable than those they actually held. I will not deal with Descartes and Hume in any great detail, but will suggest that Kenny, at any rate, has not treated them entirely fairly. I do not wish to claim that the traditional accounts of the emotions are correct, but rather that if they are misconceived, it is not for the reasons that Kenny adduces.

(4) I consider Kenny's book in particular because his is the only extended treatment of the emotions in the contemporary style. But some of his central claims seem to have been accepted by other

writers on the subject. As we have seen, he claims that the emotion: object relation is of a certain kind; he also wishes to say that necessarily all or most emotions have objects, though it is not clear if he distinguishes this claim from the first. He says that emotions are 'non-contingently connected to', or 'essentially directed to' objects. We find such claims echoed in the – not very extensive – literature: 'Emotions are very often, and perhaps always, directed towards something.'[1] 'Unlike a mood, an emotion necessarily has an object.'[2] Kenny's influence is not confined to philosophy of mind, but has spread to aesthetics. Casey, explicitly acknowledging his debt to Kenny, says: 'Emotions are . . . necessarily attached to objects.'[3] 'Emotion words are "intentional" in that they are essentially directed to objects.'[4] Casey also makes considerable use of the notion of a non-contingent connection. Like Kenny, he concludes that the object of an emotion cannot be its cause. His acceptance of Kenny's view of emotions seems integral to his theory of aesthetics.

It will be helpful if I first give a brief sketch of the general shape of Kenny's book. He begins by considering and criticising some traditional theories of the emotions, in particular those of Descartes, Locke and Hume. Among other things, he outlines their accounts of the emotion: object relation. After a chapter on experimental studies of the emotions he turns to his own theory in a chapter called 'Feelings', in which much of his discussion of objects occurs. Emotions are distinguished from other feelings, for instance from bodily sensations, primarily by virtue of the fact that they are essentially directed to objects. This also shows that there is a distinction to be made between the object of an emotion and its cause.

After dealing with motives, desire and pleasure, and outlining a theory of actions, he returns to the consideration of objects. (The chapter is called 'Objects'.) He distinguishes the 'intentional' objects of mental states from the objects of physical actions, and renews his criticism of the traditional theories, this time in terms of the Aristotelian notion of a formal object. He discusses Chisholm's suggested criteria for intentionality, and finishes the book with a theory of the will.

[1] G. Pitcher, 'Emotion', *Mind*, LXXIV (1965), p. 326.
[2] A. R. White, *The Philosophy of Mind* (New York, 1967), p. 124.
[3] J. Casey, *The Language of Criticism* (London, 1966), p. 94.
[4] *Ibid*. p. 132.

In this chapter I shall distinguish the different ends which Kenny seeks to further by his discussion of the emotion: object relation. He attempts to show something about the non-causality of the relation, the nature of emotion, and the difference between emotions and other feelings such as sensations, although these ends are inter-connected. Then in the next chapter I shall distinguish different patterns of argument that can be found in the book, and shall attempt to assess how these bear on Kenny's various ends. In saying that these patterns of argument can be distinguished, I do not mean to imply that Kenny explicitly distinguishes them.

2

Kenny's first end is the one we have previously been considering – to oppose causal theories of the emotion: object relation. More needs to be said about this, since there are various complications. Some result from Kenny's imprecise use of 'object' and 'cause', which we have already noted. This means that what he says has to be interpreted with a fair degree of latitude. But even allowing for this, there are a number of different positions which he may be attacking.

(1) There is the position which he seems to attribute to Descartes, namely that the relation of emotion to object is the simple one of effect to cause – to be the object of an emotion is just to be its cause. Clearly this would have to be modified if 'cause' is restricted to events. It is difficult to see how it would be modified, but I do not think that this matters, since it is extremely unlikely that anyone, even Descartes, could hold the thesis in this form. It would surely be necessary to impose some restriction on the kinds of causally relevant factors that could count as objects. There is no suggestion in Descartes that he thinks that the physiological causes of emotions, which he discusses at some length, are their objects, and he says nothing which commits him to this position.

(2) One might claim that the objects of emotions were some restricted sub-class of their causes, or of causally relevant factors.

(3) One might claim that the objects of emotions were causally relevant factors, but that the causation must be mediated in a certain way – perhaps through the beliefs and desires of the person who felt the emotion.

(4) One might claim that the emotion: object relation was to be

analysed wholly or partly in causal terms, without claiming that the object itself necessarily played an important part in the causal explanation of the emotion. For example, one might say that what the object of an emotion was depended on the beliefs and desires that caused the emotion, or on the desires or behaviour or tendencies to behave to which the emotion itself gave rise. The pattern of analysis might vary with the particular type of emotion and the particular type of object.

(5) Someone might accept that the emotion: object relation could not be analysed wholly in causal terms, but still wish to put forward a more limited thesis, to the effect that for some emotions and for some kinds of objects the attribution of an object to an emotion has a causal force. Thus Pears, in an article to be considered later, claims that many emotion: object statements using 'by' – 'I was amused by his remark', 'He is depressed by his lack of money', etc. – imply that the object, or in some cases some thought or belief about the object, caused the emotion or reaction in question.[5] Kenny seems committed to denying any such thesis.

(6) As we noted earlier, even if two items are related as *A* to *B*, they may be related in other ways as well.[6] In particular, even if two items are related as emotion to object, they may be related in other ways. Someone who conceded that the emotion: object relation could not be analysed causally might still wish to claim that often the object of an emotion was an important causal factor in the production of that emotion.

Kenny, however, wants to claim that there is a general distinction between the object of an emotion and its cause. He thinks that on the whole objects of emotions and causes of emotions form two mutually exclusive classes.[7] He may have overlooked the fact that there can be more than one relation between two items. That is, he may think that there is always some relation which is *the* relation between two items. Some of his formulations might naturally lead him to conclude not just that the emotion: object relation cannot be analysed in causal terms, but that an emotion cannot *be* causally related to its object. Thus he says that intentionality 'is misrepresented by Descartes, who treats the relation between a passion and its object as a contingent one of effect to cause'.[8] This may mean

---

[5] D. F. Pears, 'Causes and Objects of some Feelings and Psychological Reactions', *Ratio*, IV (1962).   [6] See Chapter III, 2.

[7] See *AEW*, pp. 71–5, 187.   [8] *Ibid.* p. 14. Cf. pp. 84, 109.

merely that it is wrong to treat the emotion: object relation as the effect: cause relation. But saying that it is wrong to treat the relation between an emotion and its object as a contingent one of effect to cause might lead one to draw the stronger conclusion that an emotion and its object *cannot* be related as effect to cause. Earlier I suggested that the move from non-contingency to non-causality might be made as follows: because the emotion: object relation is a non-contingent one, it cannot be a causal one. This concerns the analysis of the relation. There is an analogous but distinct move, which perhaps Kenny makes: because any emotion and its object are non-contingently related, they cannot be contingently related, and hence cannot be causally related.

   Against this, Kenny does allow that

It may happen on occasion that a single state of affairs is both the object and the cause of the same emotion; for while a man *need* not know the cause of his emotions, he *may* do so. Thus, when a man feels depressed because of his failing health, his debility is both the object and the cause of his feeling of depression.[9]

This suggests that Kenny may not view the classes of objects and causes as completely exclusive. However, he clearly conceives of this as a rather peculiar and exceptional case, and he may just be being inconsistent. Whether or not Kenny adheres to the second variant of the argument, other philosophers seem to have done so, or at least to have arrived at the equivalently strong conclusion that desires, for instance, *cannot* be causally related to their manifestations in behaviour.

   It may be unfair to claim that Kenny attributes the first position unqualified to Descartes. He says that 'in general, Descartes treats the relation of the object of fear to fear itself as being that of cause to effect',[10] and, generalising, that Descartes misrepresented the intentionality of the emotions, treating 'the relation between a passion and its object as a contingent one of effect to cause'.[11] Later he mentions cases where the object of the emotion is in the future, and therefore cannot be its cause. He says that in these cases

a Cartesian might say that dread of the next war, for example, is caused not by the next war, but by the image of the next war. But this

[9] *Ibid*. p. 75.   [10] *Ibid*. pp. 10–11.   [11] *Ibid*. p. 14.

is already to admit that the object of an emotion differs from its cause . . .[12]

This implies that to admit that the object of an emotion differs from its cause contradicts the general Cartesian theory of objects, but it is compatible with allowing that Descartes placed some restrictions on the types of causes which counted as objects. However, Kenny does not explicitly make this qualification. He argues that whereas Descartes confused the object of an emotion with its cause, it is important to keep them apart. Since he does not acknowledge that a wide variety of factors may be causally relevant to the production of any effect, he does not discuss the suggestion that although the object of an emotion would not naturally be picked out as the cause of that emotion, yet it may still be causally relevant in some way, and owe its status as object to this causal relevance.

Descartes seems in fact to have no explicit general view of the emotion: object relation. But what he says about the particular passions suggests that if he had made a general view explicit, it would not have been of the first form, but probably of the third or fourth. Consider one or two instances.

Love is an emotion of the soul caused by the movement of the spirits which incites it to join itself willingly to objects which appear to it to be agreeable. And hatred is an emotion caused by the spirits which incite the soul to desire to be separated from the objects which present themselves to it as hurtful.[13]

Derision or scorn is a sort of joy mingled with hatred, which proceeds from our perceiving some small evil in a person whom we consider deserving of it.[14]

Gratitude is also a species of love excited in us by some action on the part of him for whom we have it, by which also we believe that he has done us some good or at least had that intention.[15]

These definitions may appear somewhat quaint, but that is not the point. The object of love for Descartes is clearly that which appears to the soul agreeable, and to which it joins itself willingly. The object of derision is the person in whom some small evil is

---

[12] *Ibid.* p. 72.

[13] R. Descartes, *The Passions of the Soul*, II, lxxix, in E. S. Haldane and G. R. T. Ross (translators), *The Philosophical Works of Descartes* (2 vols., Cambridge, England, 1911), Vol. I.

[14] *Ibid.* III, clxxviii.   [15] *Ibid.* III, cxciii.

perceived. Descartes may think that perceiving the evil in the person causes the derision, and that it is by virtue of this that the person is the object of the derision, but this is not just to think that the object of the derision is its cause. To represent Descartes as *simply* confusing the object of an emotion with its cause would surely be unfair.

Kenny admits that Hume distinguishes between the object of an emotion and its cause, but says that for Hume, too, the relation between an emotion and its object is a contingent one. It is plausible to say that for at least some passions, Hume's view is similar to the fourth position outlined above. Thus in connection with pride he says that we have 'a passion placed betwixt two ideas, of which the one produces it, and the other is produced by it. The first idea, therefore, represents the *cause*, the second the *object* of the passion'.[16] Thus the object of pride is self, since pride always gives rise to an idea of self. Hume's view would, then, still qualify as a causal theory of the object of pride. But it is not so clear that his account of the objects of love and hatred, say, can be read along these lines.

3

Kenny thinks that someone who holds the traditional view of the emotions cannot give an adequate account of the emotion: object relation, and that this provides a reason for rejecting the view supplementary to the other considerations he adduces. To show this is the second end of his discussion. It partly overlaps with the first, but is more comprehensive. Hume, according to Kenny, distinguished the object of an emotion from its cause, but still thought that the connection between an emotion and its object was contingent. Hume's view also must be mistaken if the emotion: object relation can be shown to be non-contingent.

Kenny characterises the traditional view as the view that emotions are 'purely private mental events', or 'internal impressions', or 'events directly observable only by the person who experiences them'. Kenny denies that such a view is correct, but I do not think that he wishes to say that emotions are directly observable to others in the way in which a smile, say, is directly observable to others.

[16] D. Hume, *A Treatise of Human Nature* (Oxford, 1888), II, I, 2.

He is not a behaviourist. What is at issue is not so much the internality or externality of mental states in any literal sense, as the nature of the criteria according to which they are classified or assigned to kinds. Kenny seems to think that Descartes and Hume would have said that for a mental state to belong to a certain kind – for example, to be a pain, or a feeling of fear – is for it to have a certain introspectible feature, and that it can be the kind of mental state it is, and can be identified as being of that kind, without regard to such public phenomena as its cause and its manifestation in behaviour. Furthermore, he thinks that on this view an emotion can be the kind of emotion it is regardless of the nature of its object. He argues – correctly – that the criteria for the application of emotion terms are at least partly behavioural, and also that emotions impose restrictions on the kinds of objects that they can take. This is one of his reasons for claiming that the connection between emotions and their objects is a non-contingent one.

It is interesting to compare Kenny's critique of the traditional view of the emotions with that of another philosopher of the same school, Bedford.[17] Kenny claims that, contrary to the traditional view, emotions are not internal impressions or purely private mental events. Bedford uses very similar arguments in support of his claim that, contrary to the traditional view, emotions are not sensations, feelings, or experiences. But Kenny cannot claim that these arguments have shown that emotions are not sensations, feelings, or experiences, for according to him sensations, feelings, and experiences are not internal impressions or purely private mental events either – they, too, are non-contingently connected to their manifestations in behaviour. Indeed Kenny wants to say that emotions *are* feelings, or at least sometimes are feelings. (He draws a distinction between emotions as feelings and emotions as motives.) How he distinguishes between emotions and other feelings we shall see in the next section.

Kenny invokes the intentionality of the emotions against those psychologists who equate emotions with physiological processes: 'There is a conceptual connection also between a feeling and its object, whereas the physiological processes studied by psychologists lack intentionality'.[18] He also uses it against behaviourism.[19] Here

---

[17] E. Bedford, 'Emotions', *Proceedings of the Aristotelian Society*, LVI (1955–6).

[18] *AEW*, p. 38. [19] *Ibid*. p. 191.

we have a particular example of the way philosophers appeal to intentionality to show that the mental cannot be reduced to the physical.[20]

4

The third purpose of Kenny's discussion of the emotion: object relation is to give a criterion for distinguishing emotions from other feelings such as bodily sensations. Unlike Bedford, he seems to think that emotions are items of the same type as sensations. They are both kinds of feelings, where, it seems, anything is a feeling if we use the verb 'feel' in reporting it. He begins the 'Feelings' chapter by distinguishing various uses of 'feel'. This verb can be followed by a direct object, by an adjective, or by an *oratio obliqua* clause. He draws a distinction between 'those reports of feelings in which the direct object is replaceable by an adjective, and those in which it corresponds to a that-clause' which 'enables us to see through the *prima facie* similarity between emotions and perceptions'. Thus on the one hand, 'to feel anger may be to feel angry, but to feel a lump is not to feel lumpish. Feeling fear does not differ from feeling afraid, but feeling the earth is not at all the same as feeling earthy'.[21] On the other hand, 'to feel the lump on the mattress is to feel that there is a lump on the mattress; to feel the heat of the fire is to feel that the fire is hot', whereas 'if one feels guilt, then one feels guilty; but it does not follow that one feels that one is guilty, for one may regard one's guilt-feeling as the quite irrational consequence of an innocent action, due perhaps to a hangover from childish tabus'.[22] However, this

does not by itself provide a criterion for distinguishing feelings of emotion from all other feelings. Hunger is not an emotion, though to feel hunger is to feel hungry and is not necessarily to feel that one is hungry . . . In general, therefore, our criterion distinguishes between

---

[20] See Chapter xv, below.   [21] *AEW*, p. 53.

[22] *Ibid*. p. 54. Many of Kenny's specific equations seem to me dubious, but I shall not pursue this, as I am unhappy about his method. At least he has not given it a sufficient rationale. Does the fact that there is a *prima facie* similarity between reports of perceptions and reports of emotions, for instance, show that there is a *prima facie* similarity between perceptions and emotions?

emotions and sensations on the one hand, and perceptions on the other. It does not, in general, distinguish between emotions and sensations.[23]

Again, emotions are distinguished from perceptions but not from sensations in that there are organs of perception. However, one respect in which emotions differ from sensations is that emotions are not localised. Another is that emotions have a characteristic history. 'Any pattern is accidental to a sensation, while some pattern is essential to an emotion.'[24] This point is not elaborated sufficiently to be useful, nor does Kenny say anything in its support as a general claim. He does not think, anyway, that either of these is the chief difference between emotions and sensations. 'The most important difference between a sensation and an emotion is that emotions, unlike sensations, are essentially directed to objects.'[25]

Even if the fact that emotions but not sensations have objects is an important difference between them, the way in which Kenny puts his claim causes a feeling of uneasiness, and in particular the way in which he seems to treat this fact as an isolated fact about emotions and sensations. There are two distinct points here.

(1) Kenny may mean that the most important difference between emotions and sensations is that the former are essentially directed to objects, whereas the latter, even if they are directed to objects, are not essentially directed to objects. But it can't be an isolated fact about emotions that they are essentially directed to objects. If it were, we would have to be able to say of an emotion E and a sensation S: 'It happens that S has an object, but it differs from E in that it doesn't *have* to have an object.' This is impossible: modal properties can't exist in isolation.[26]

(2) Alternatively, the 'most important difference' might be meant to be just that emotions have objects and sensations do not. But even if this is what Kenny means, he would still be treating the fact that emotions have objects as an isolated fact about them – as if emotions and sensations were much the same kind of item, the emotions being those which had objects, the sensations being those which lacked them – when clearly it isn't an isolated fact about them, but results from and is bound up with other features of the emotions which differentiate them from sensations.

In the next chapter I will explore further what exactly is intended by this claim.

[23] *Ibid.* pp. 54–5.   [24] *Ibid.* p. 60.   [25] *Ibid.*
[26] I owe this point to J. F. Bennett.

V

Kenny's arguments

I

Kenny's first argument occurs in the 'Feelings' chapter.[1] He states the important difference between sensations and emotions, and then, we must presume, adduces considerations in support of his claim:

The most important difference between a sensation and an emotion is that emotions, unlike sensations, are essentially directed to objects. It is possible to be hungry without being hungry for anything in particular, as it is not possible to be ashamed without being ashamed of anything in particular. It is possible to be in pain without knowing what is hurting one, as it is not possible to be delighted without knowing what is delighting one. It is not in general possible to ascribe a piece of behaviour or a sensation to a particular emotional state without at the same time ascribing an object to the emotion. If a man runs past me I can say nothing about his emotions unless I know whether he is running away from A or running towards B; no flutterings of the heart or meltings of the bowels could tell me I was in love without telling me with whom.

He then suggests an objection which might be thought to show that the emotion: object connection was purely contingent:

But are there not objectless emotions, such as pointless depression and undirected fears? And does not their existence show that the connection between an emotion and its object is purely contingent? There are indeed such emotions, though some emotions often described as objectless are not so in fact.

He replies to the objection by saying that although there may be cases of emotions lacking objects, these are in some sense parasitic upon emotions with objects. Thus neurotic fear may be objectless, but 'The use of the word "fear" in such cases is . . . dependent upon its use in cases where fear has an object.' This enables him to conclude that 'Despite such cases . . . the connection between emotions

[1] *AEW*, p. 60–2.

and their objects is not a contingent one. The philosophers considered earlier consistently neglected this fact . . . [The emotion] was not related, except causally, to any object of its own.'

I will consider this first from the point of view of non-contingency and anti-causality, and then from the point of view of the distinction between emotions and sensations.

(1) I have claimed that philosophers who have supported anti-causal theses by appeal to non-contingency have moved illegitimately from saying that it is non-contingent *that* there is a certain connection to saying that the connection itself is of a certain kind – it is a non-contingent one. I must show that this is what Kenny has done.

The conclusion, and the reference to the earlier discussion of the traditional philosophers, indicate that the whole passage is supposed to establish some thesis about the nature of the emotion : object connection. But the considerations adduced in the first paragraph seem only to support some thesis about the universality of the connection. In fact each sentence in the paragraph makes a different claim, but the most plausible way to take the whole is as showing that emotions must have objects, whereas sensations needn't have. If we stop here, nothing follows of an anti-causal kind. This thesis about the universality, or scope, of the emotion : object connection does not entail, and is not entailed by, any thesis about the nature of the connection. If all emotions must have objects, it does not follow that the relation of an emotion to its object is not a causal one, any more than it follows from the fact that all causes must have effects that the relation of a cause to its effect is not a causal one. Conversely, if it made sense to talk of a non-contingent connection as a kind of connection, it might be false that emotions must have objects, but true that when an emotion did have an object, the connection between it and its object was a non-contingent one. Kenny can surely only think that he has established anything about the nature of the emotion : object connection if he has made a conflation of the kind I suggested. In this case what has enabled him to do this is probably his use of the dangerous word 'essentially'.

Our suspicions are confirmed by the way Kenny handles the supposed objection to his claim. One can see how the existence of objectless emotions would refute a claim about the scope of the emotion : object relation – and also how it would seem to remove the possibility of giving this kind of criterion for distinguishing emotions from sensations – but why should it be thought to show anything about the nature of the relation between an emotion and its object in those cases where the emotion does have an object? Why, for instance, does Kenny think that someone might see the existence of objectless emotions as letting in the possibility that the connection between an emotion and its object is only a causal one? Surely the only explanation is that Kenny has conflated the claim that it is contingent that an emotion has an object with the claim that the connection between an emotion and its object is a contingent (and thus possibly a causal) one.

Kenny's answer to the objection complicates matters even further, for now his claim is transformed from one about particular emotion-instances into one about emotion-types. That is, it is no longer a claim about what must be true in any particular case of fear, anger, shame, etc., but rather a claim about fear, anger, shame, etc., understood as types of emotions. He now allows that there can be objectless emotion-instances, particular emotions lacking objects, but says that for an emotion-type instances of that type lacking objects are necessarily exceptional, parasitic upon instances of that type with objects. For a type of phenomenon to be a type of emotion, the central instances of that type must have objects. Talk of non-contingency is still in place here, for if what he says is correct it is not contingent that the central instances of any emotion-type have objects. But still nothing has been said about the nature of the connection in those cases where it does exist.

Furthermore, surely nothing has been said which Descartes can reasonably be accused of neglecting. Descartes says nothing which suggests that the emotion:object connection is not universal. He says nothing general about the emotion:object connection at all. Perhaps Descartes failed to point out that all or most emotions must have objects, but I do not think that his discussion suffered from this. By the same token, it is very odd that Kenny should credit Descartes with having 'raised, often for the first time, genuine questions which since his day have figured in every discussion of the emotions . . . [for instance] the problem of objectless emotions such as *Angst*, which exercised Freud and Wittgenstein'.[2] Descartes does not seem to say anything on this point at all.

Although more could be said about Kenny's centrality thesis,

[2] *Ibid*. pp. 16–17.

which might be taken in a number of different ways, it does not seem necessary to do so. However it is taken, it will not support an anti-causal claim. It seems to me clear that Kenny thinks that he has established something about the nature of the emotion: object connection which conflicts with what the traditional philosophers said, that the considerations he adduces concern the scope of the emotion: object connection, or the status of the claim that all or most emotions have objects, and that it is only by an illegitimate move that he gets from one to the other. I may have misunderstood this passage, but I do not see how else it is to be interpreted.

(2) What exactly is the difference between emotions and sensations supposed to be? It cannot be that all emotions have objects and no sensations do, for Kenny thinks that hunger is a sensation, and hunger can have an object. He may mean that emotions are feelings of a kind such that instances of that kind must have objects, whereas sensations are feelings of a kind such that instances of that kind may have objects, but need not. But this would presuppose some prior way of assigning feelings to the kinds in question, which would surely provide a *more* important difference between sensations and emotions.

Perhaps the difference is supposed to be not between any feeling which is an emotion and any feeling which is a sensation, but between any *type* of feeling which is a type of emotion and any *type* of feeling which is a type of sensation. If a feeling-type is an emotion-type, then all instances – or, in view of his reply to the objection, central instances – of that type must have objects, whereas if a feeling-type is a sensation-type, instances – even central instances – of that type need not have objects. The immediate objection is that for Kenny hunger is a sensation, and hunger must be for food. Kenny's notion of an object is so general that he must admit that this qualifies. In the present context the second sentence of the first extract quoted in this chapter is of interest, for it suggests that the relevant fact about emotions is not that they are directed towards objects as such, but that they are directed towards particular objects. However, this does not seem to be generally true. Even if I can't be ashamed without being ashamed of some particular item, I can be afraid without being afraid of some particular item. Thus I can be afraid of earthquakes even if there is no particular earthquake of which I am afraid. Perhaps Kenny would claim that this kind of fear is also parasitic upon fear of particular items, but if this is true, it requires much more argument to show it to be true.

Kenny would probably say that the important difference between an emotion and a sensation is not that any emotion has an object and no sensation has, but that the connection between an emotion and its object is of a certain kind, namely non-contingent, whereas the connection between a sensation and its object, if it has one, is not of this kind. But as we have seen, he has not succeeded in showing anything about the nature of the emotion: object relation.

Before we go on to consider Kenny's next argument, certain general points need to be made. First, the artificiality of some of the preceding discussion suggests that we have a perfectly good distinction between emotions and sensations which does not depend on the fact that the former have objects and the latter do not. Otherwise, rather than wriggling around in the attempt to exclude hunger, why not just admit that hunger is an emotion? Secondly, Kenny's only criterion for something being a feeling seems to be that we use the verb 'feel' in reporting it. But we often speak of feeling desires, inclinations, impulses, urges, and so on. If his criterion is supposed to distinguish emotions from anything else which could be called a feeling – and he does seem to be aiming to delimit the class of emotions – appeal to intentionality surely won't do, since desires, inclinations, etc., might similarly be claimed to be intentional. Thirdly, Kenny gives no general arguments in support of his thesis that all emotions have objects. Such general arguments could presumably be of two kinds – either some kind of enumerative argument to show that his claim was in fact true of all emotions (but this would presuppose some independent way of picking out emotions), or a conceptual argument to show that if anything is to count as an emotion it must have an object. Kenny attempts neither of these. His procedure here, as elsewhere, is to generalise from one or two instances. But this, though perhaps a fertile way of suggesting general philosophical theses, is hardly a satisfactory way of establishing them.

2

The second pattern of argument occurs in Kenny's discussion of the traditional philosophers, and then again in the 'Objects' chapter, but not, curiously enough, in the 'Feelings' chapter. It is distinct from the pattern of argument considered in the previous section, though Kenny does not make this clear.

Kenny acknowledges that Hume drew a distinction between the object and the cause of an emotion, then asks whether for Hume the connection between an emotion and its object is contingent or necessary. He quotes in answer a passage from Hume which shows, he asserts, that the connection being affirmed is a contingent one. His grounds for saying this are that on Hume's view

it is because our minds happen to be made as they are that the object of pride is self, not because of anything involved in the concept of *pride* . . . An examination of pride itself, therefore, could no more teach us that it was connected with the idea of self than an *a priori* examination of a stone could show that it would fall downward if unsupported. It always happens that we feel proud of our own achievements and not, say, of the industry of ants in stone-age Papua . . . The idea of self is not part of the nature of pride and humility; all that belongs to this is a particular experience.[3]

In opposition to this, Kenny wishes to claim that there are logical restrictions on the type of object which each emotion can have.

In fact, each of the emotions is appropriate – logically, and not just morally appropriate – only to certain restricted objects. One cannot be afraid of just anything, nor happy about anything whatsoever . . . What is not possible is to be grateful for, or proud of, something which one regards as an evil unmixed with good. Again, it is possible to be envious of one's own fruit trees; but only if one mistakenly believes that the land on which they stand is part of one's neighbour's property . . . What is not possible is to envy something which one believes to belong to oneself.[4]

What Kenny is claiming is that a particular emotion can only be a case of pride, or fear, or envy, if it has a certain kind of object. It is not a contingent fact that one is only proud of what one thinks to be in some way connected with oneself. Now if this were true, what would it show about the nature of the connection between an emotion and its object, and what would it show about the nature of emotions themselves?

(1) Kenny thinks that this shows that Hume was wrong to treat the emotion: object connection as a contingent one. But if he thinks

[3] *Ibid*. pp. 24–5.   [4] *Ibid*. pp. 192–3.

that he has established something about the nature of the emotion: object connection, as he seems to do, he has once more taken a non-contingent fact about connections to be a fact about non-contingent connections. Whereas in his first argument the non-contingent fact about connections was the fact that all or most emotions are connected to objects, here it is the fact that for any emotion-type, emotions of that type are connected to objects of a certain type. But although the starting-point is different, the move is the same, and is no more legitimate here than in the earlier context.

Kenny's point is really one about the basis of classification of emotions. If he is correct, one of the conditions that a particular emotion must satisfy to count as a case of pride is that it should have a certain kind of object. But as we have seen, there is no reason why items should not be classified in causal terms. This is brought out rather neatly by one of Kenny's own contrasts. He says at one point that 'A feeling of anxiety is non-contingently related to the alarming circumstances which give rise to it; the relation between dyspepsia and its cause is purely contingent.'[5] But the criteria for the presence of many types of illness are partly causal, and I think that this goes for dyspepsia as well.[6]

I suggested earlier that Kenny may think that in saying that the emotion: object relation is non-contingent, he has said *what* the emotion: object relation is. Now an analysis of the emotion: object relation will tell what determines what the object of a particular emotion is. It will tell us how to find the object of any emotion. Suppose that Kenny says that the object of a particular case of fear is the particular item to which that fear is non-contingently connected. This won't do, for what he has established by his argument, if anything, is really about the connection between *types* of emotion and *types* of object. He might transform his claim into one about particular emotions and particular objects, by saying that any emotion of a certain type must have an object of a certain type. But this leaves completely unsettled the question of *which* instance of the latter type is the object of a particular instance of the former type. Even if an instance of fear has to have as object a ø item, it may not have to have as object the particular ø item that it does.

[5] *Ibid.* p. 84.
[6] Cf. H. Putnam, 'Brains and Behaviour', in R. J. Butler (ed.), *Analytical Philosophy II* (Oxford, 1965).

So Kenny has said nothing about the connection between a particular emotion and its particular object, or what determines which particular object a particular emotion is connected to.

(2) In asking what this claim shows about the nature of the emotions, we should consider it in conjunction with Kenny's parallel claim that emotions are non-contingently connected to their manifestations in behaviour. This could also be construed as a point about the basis of classification of emotions – that we classify emotions as fear, anger, etc., partly on the basis of the kind of behaviour to which they give rise. Now if these claims about the basis of classification of emotions, or the criteria for applying emotion-terms, are true, it follows that in Kenny's rather special sense the emotions are not internal impressions or purely private mental events. But Kenny sees his thesis as contradicting Descartes and Hume, and also incidentally the behaviourist psychologists.

Descartes and Hume, with the philosophers and psychologists who followed them, treated the relationship between an emotion and its formal object, which is a logical one, as if it were a contingent matter of fact. If the emotions were internal impressions or behaviour patterns, there would be no logical restrictions on the type of object which each emotion could have. It would be a mere matter of fact that people were not angered by being benefited . . .[7]

Kenny thinks that what he says contradicts Descartes and Hume, because he thinks that they held that emotions were internal impressions in his sense. But it is not clear that Descartes would have denied what Kenny says about the basis of classification of the emotions. He gives a series of what he calls 'Definitions' of the passions. He thinks that there are six primary passions. Now for Kenny an internal impression is one which is defined in terms of internal features, without reference to anything public, such as its object, or the kind of behaviour to which it gives rise. But Descartes' definitions of his primary passions do not seem to be of this kind. Thus consider his definition of love already quoted: 'Love is an emotion of the soul caused by the movement of the spirits which incites it to join itself willingly to objects which appear to it to be agreeable.' It is surely reasonable to take this as defining love at least partly in terms of the behaviour it tends to produce. Descartes defines the secondary passions in terms of the primary

[7] *AEW*, p. 191.

passions; the former are sub-species and combinations of the latter. The differentiating factors are such features as the kinds of thoughts and desires which produce them, and the kinds of desires and behaviour which they in turn produce. Thus:

Pity is a species of sadness, mingled with love or good-will towards those whom we see suffering some evil of which we consider them undeserving.[8]

Shame . . . is a species of sadness, also founded on self-love, which proceeds from the apprehension or the fear which we possess of being blamed.[9]

See also the definitions cited in Chapter IV, 2.

It might be argued that Descartes' use of 'definition' differs from ours, and that his aim is simply to give a factual account of the passions – to say what as a matter of fact causes a certain passion, and what kind of behaviour it as a matter of fact gives rise to – rather than to undertake a conceptual elucidation. Against this is the fact that he does not give any other account of what the emotion words mean, or what the criteria are in respect of which we apply them.[10]

Hume, of course, said that

The passions of PRIDE and HUMILITY being simple and uniform impressions, 'tis impossible we can ever, by a multitude of words, give a just definition of them, or indeed of any of the passions. The utmost we can pretend to is a description of them, by an enumeration of such circumstances, as attend them: But as these words, *pride* and *humility*, are of general use, and the impressions they represent the most common of any, every one, of himself, will be able to form a just idea of them, without any danger of mistake.[11]

Hume equates the meaning of a word with the corresponding idea. We can make sense of this passage if we take him as thinking that the idea corresponding to the word 'pride' is just the passion itself, or perhaps some idea resembling the impression which pride strictly

---

[8] Descartes, *The Passions of the Soul*, III, clxxxv.   [9] *Ibid*. ccv.

[10] His only other extensive use of 'definition' is in the appendix to the 'Replies to the Second Objections', and there it seems to correspond fairly well with present use. I do not myself think that a clear distinction can be drawn between factual account and conceptual elucidation.

[11] Hume, *Treatise*, II, I, 2.

speaking is. Then anyone who has felt pride will *ipso facto* know the meaning of 'pride'.

However, Descartes does not say anything of this sort. This may be because, unlike Hume, he did not have an explicit theory of meaning. Perhaps if he had had an explicit theory of meaning, it would have been like Hume's, and perhaps if he had had a theory of meaning like Hume's, he would have said what Hume says about the meaning of emotion words. It seems somewhat arbitrary, however, to assume that Descartes would have made the same mistake as Hume if he had thought of it.

3

As I said at the end of Chapter iii, 4 above, some passages in Kenny suggest that he may wish to advance an argument connected with the identification of emotions. He claims that the Cartesian theses would have been rejected by Descartes' predecessors. 'The denial of the intentionality of the emotions runs counter to the Aristotelian commonplace that the passions are specified by their objects.'[12] Later he uses a similar form of words: 'Causes are assigned to particular emotions, and objects to unspecified emotions; this is because emotions are specified by their objects.'[13] He also says that 'It is not in general possible to identify an emotion without identifying its object.'[14]

We might take this as another variant of the argument that an emotion of a certain kind must have an object of a certain kind, that is, that to know what emotion someone is feeling one must know what *kind* of object it has. (The Aristotelian reference would suggest this, since Aristotle is later represented as claiming that emotions have formal objects, i.e. that there are restrictions on what kind of object an emotion can take.) But one could also take the claim another way, and the last passage especially suggests that it should be so taken, namely as a claim about identification proper. The claim would then be that in some sense one cannot identify an emotion without referring to its *particular* object. This is clearly a different claim to the claim that one cannot identify an emotion without knowing what *kind* of object it has.

[12] *AEW*, p. 16.   [13] *Ibid*. p. 73.   [14] *Ibid*. p. 64.

But what is meant by talk of 'identifying' someone's emotion? Perhaps *A* counts as having identified *B*'s emotion if he knows *what* emotion *B* is feeling. But how stringent demands we put on *A*'s knowledge before allowing that he knows what emotion *B* is feeling seems to vary with the particular context. There may be some contexts in which *A* would not be said to know what *B* was feeling if he knew *only* that he was angry or afraid – where we would demand that *A* know the object of *B*'s anger or fear. But this does not seem to be generally the case. We often allow that *A* knows what emotion *B* is feeling even if all he knows is that *B* is afraid. That is, if 'identify' is taken this way, knowledge of the object is not generally, though it may be sometimes, considered necessary.

What Kenny intends may not be precisely this. He may mean that one cannot in general *tell* what emotion someone is feeling without knowing what its object is. Here part of the first passage quoted in Section 1 of this chapter seems relevant:

It is not in general possible to ascribe a piece of behaviour or a sensation to a particular emotional state without at the same time ascribing an object to the emotion. If a man runs past me I can say nothing about his emotions unless I know whether he is running away from A or running towards B; no flutterings of the heart or meltings of the bowels could tell me I was in love without telling me with whom.[15]

This perhaps supports the present interpretation. However, it is surely misleading to assimilate the first-person to the third-person case as Kenny does. Perhaps I cannot find out what emotion I am feeling without finding out what its object is, though this is arguable. But I can certainly find out what emotion someone else is feeling without finding out what its object is. For instance, I can often see that someone is afraid without knowing what he is afraid of. Besides, if we allow the other person to talk, he can always tell me what emotion he is feeling without telling me what its object is.

However, 'identify' might be understood another way. Although Kenny may not have intended his claim this way, if it is so taken it becomes quite interesting. In this sense, to identify an item is to pick out the item in order to talk about it. One might talk of an identifying description – a description which picks out only one item.

[15] *Ibid.* p. 60.

There are some identifying descriptions which as a matter of fact pick out only one item – if the world had been otherwise they would have picked out more. There are others which necessarily pick out at most one item. Thus the description 'dog born at sea' may as a matter of fact pick out a unique item, but there is no guarantee that it does not pick out two, or two hundred. On the other hand the description 'first dog born at sea ever' can pick out one item at most – it has a built-in guarantee of uniqueness.

Consider now the case of emotions. The description '*A*'s fear at time *t*' may as a matter of fact pick out only one fear, but there is no guarantee that this is so. Someone can have several fears at the same time. What is necessary to ensure that one fear at most is being described? It seems reasonable to say that a reference to the object of the fear is sufficient. Although someone can have more than one fear at a time, he cannot have more than one fear of *B*'s dog at a time. It is, it might be argued, a necessary (though perhaps not a sufficient) condition of someone's having two fears at a time that he should be afraid of two different objects at that time. In this sense fears would be distinguished by their objects, and to be sure of having made an identifying description of a fear one would have to mention its object. Perhaps this claim could be generalised to cover other emotions as well.[16]

As will emerge later, I think that it is false that we cannot identify an emotion in this sense without identifying its object. If it were true, that is, if the *only* way in which emotions could be identified were by reference to their objects, this might show that the emotion: object relation cannot be analysed in causal terms. For surely if someone has two different fears at the same time, these must be distinguished by some *present* difference. They could not differ *only* in that they were caused in different ways. It would follow that either the possession of an object by an emotion is a fact about the *present* nature of the emotion, and thus is not a causal fact about it, or that, contrary to what the argument claimed, there is some way of identifying emotions other than by reference to their objects.

I think that the latter alternative is the correct one. That is, I

[16] One difficulty is this: although we can talk of *a* fear, *a* hope, we have no comparable way of talking in the case of other emotions such as anger. If someone is angry with two different people at the same time, what does he have two of?

think that the attribution of an object to an emotion does in general have a causal force. However, I do not think that to attribute an object to an emotion is *just* to say something about the causal history of the emotion. Regardless of the question of identification, it seems plausible to say that in attributing an object to an emotion one implies something about the present nature of the emotion, that is, that two emotions with different objects differ not solely in their causal genesis. Furthermore, if the present nature of an emotion varies with its object, then the fact that emotions can take a wide variety of objects may impose some restrictions on the kind of item an emotion can be. For example, fear can be felt of any number of different things. If fear of any two objects must differ in some non-causal way, this tells us something about the kind of state fear must be. In particular, it may point to some important difference between emotions and sensations such as pain, whose present nature does not vary in the appropriate way.

If emotions were only identifiable in terms of their objects, would this show that they were non-contingently connected to their objects? Although Kenny does not explicitly use this argument in support of his claim, someone might argue as follows: For a person to have the emotion he does, his emotion must have the particular object it does, for otherwise it would have been a different emotion. For it to have been *that* emotion, it had to have *that* object. Thus in some sense it is necessary for an emotion's being the emotion it is that it have the object it does. This might be taken to show that there is a non-contingent connection between the emotion and its object. However, even if we allowed the claim that it was in some sense necessary that *this* emotion should have had *this* object – which seems to be entirely dubious – the move to talk of a non-contingent connection would be no more legitimate than in the cases considered previously.

4

Kenny has another argument to support his claim that the emotion : object relation is not to be analysed causally, which concerns the nature of one's knowledge of the objects of one's own emotions. It does not depend on showing that the emotion : object relation is a non-contingent one. I think that I have covered everything that

Kenny has to say on this topic. I hope that I have shown that he has arrived at talk of non-contingent connections only by way of an illegitimate route of the kind suggested in Chapter III, that none of the arguments considered so far cast doubt on the causal nature of the emotion: object relation, and that the Cartesian theory of the emotions cannot be dismissed as easily as Kenny thinks.

I shall consider Kenny's further argument in connection with a related discussion by Pears in Chapters XII and XIII. I shall have occasion to return to some of the positive aspects of Kenny's discussion, such as the suggestion that it is a very important fact about emotions that they have objects, and the claim that there are restrictions on the kinds of objects that emotions can take. But first I must subject the notion of the object of an emotion to a closer scrutiny.

VI

Objects: delimitation of scope

I

My main concern so far has been to rebut a major objection in principle to the use of causal concepts in analysing the emotion: object relation. The objection rested on the claim that emotions are non-contingently connected to their objects. I have argued that there is no coherent notion of a non-contingent connection which will render the objection valid. I will argue later that the other main anti-causal argument is equally invalid. In the meantime I will assume that there is no general bar to the use of causal concepts in this area.

Hitherto I have talked casually and uncritically of the objects of emotions. Now I must attempt to make the notion more precise. Clearly we have a rough idea of what this notion is, for when Kenny talks generally about objects of emotions, he does not leave us completely at a loss. We feel we know the kind of thing he has in mind. However if the notion is going to play an important part in our discussion, we must sharpen our idea of how it works.

To attain greater precision, we must do two things. First, we must delimit the scope of the term 'object'. We must decide exactly what it is to apply to. Secondly, we must provide a rationale for the notion. We must justify its use, by showing that it is legitimate and illuminating to refer generally to the objects of emotions. It will not suffice simply to say that the term 'object' applies in such-and-such cases. We have to show that these cases are importantly similar. We must make clear what in general is meant by saying that an emotion has an object, what determines what the object of a particular emotion is, when an emotion and an item in the world are related as emotion to object.

2

This undertaking is necessary, if only because Gosling, in criticising Kenny, has claimed that Kenny 'has no concept of object which at all serves his purposes, though he does have one which prevents him from seeing the complexity of the situation',[1] and indeed that 'the concept of an object is more or less useless for Kenny's purposes'.[2] I do not think that Gosling is right. Rather, I think that the notion of an object can be clarified into a useful working tool. However, as I shall be using the term, its scope will be more restricted than some of Kenny's theses require. It will not be true, for instance, that all emotions have objects, or even that those which lack objects are dependent on those which have them in the strong sense that Kenny suggests.

Philosophers did not entirely invent the notion of the object of an emotion. The general use of 'object' can be seen as a philosophical extension of everyday speech, for we do sometimes ordinarily talk of objects of emotions. Thus we might naturally say 'The unfortunate object of his wrath cowered in the corner'. We might similarly talk of the object of someone's fear, or pity, or love. I do not think we would naturally talk of the object of someone's embarrassment, or shame, or grief, or repentance. I think we would tend to use 'object' in everyday speech only when the emotion is concerned with a particular person or thing. (The phrase 'concerned with' is a vague one – part of our purpose is to clarify it.) But whether or not ordinary use is as restricted as I suggest is not very important.

I wish to use the term 'object' to apply to items in the world of any category, and not just to particular persons or things. That is, I wish it to apply to items such as the following –

(i) events: a person can be overjoyed at the return of his son, or horrified by a catastrophe;

(ii) states or conditions of persons or things: a person can be annoyed by the untidiness of the garden, or worried about his wife's continued illness;

(iii) attributes or qualities of people: a person can be overawed by someone's intelligence, or envious of someone's happiness;

[1] J. C. B. Gosling, 'Emotion and Object', *Philosophical Review*, LXXIV (1965), p. 486.　　[2] *Ibid*. p. 500.

(iv) relationships: a person can be jealous of his wife's friendship with another man;

(v) actions or behaviour: a person can be ashamed of the way he treated his parents, or embarrassed by someone's bad manners.

Some emotions seem to be primarily concerned with particular persons or things – fear, anger, hate, love, pity, envy, etc. Some seem to be primarily reactions to events or actions, to what has happened or to what someone has done – shame, embarrassment, remorse, joy, regret, etc. I do not mean to suggest that emotions are sharply divided into two classes, for some can be viewed in either way. Thus gratitude can be viewed as a concern with a person or as a reaction to something the person has done, and the same is true of other emotions.

As I said above, restriction of 'object' to items in the world means that Kenny's claim that all, or central, cases of emotions have objects cannot be sustained. But some of the points that he wants to make can be reformulated in terms of the broader notion of intentionality. Philosophers have used 'intentionality' to refer to a more extensive range of phenomena than does my notion of possession of an object. They have claimed that beliefs, desires, etc., which do not normally have objects in my sense, are intentional.[3] If this broader notion of intentionality is valid in its own right, Kenny may be able to claim that all or central cases of emotions are intentional. I will suggest in Chapter xv that there is a valid notion of intentionality such that nearly all emotions are intentional, and such that beliefs, desires, etc., are intentional also.

I will now outline some cases of emotions which, as I am using the term, do not have objects. I hope that the justification for using the term in this restricted way will emerge in the course of the discussion.

3

(1) Sometimes an emotion is founded on a mistaken existential belief. A person's mental state is just as it would be if he felt an emotion for an item in the world, but no item of the relevant kind exists. We can give some examples:

(a) Smith, a soft-hearted fellow, is approached by a beggar, who

[3] Although some desires may – one can want a specific object.

spins him a harrowing tale of his wife's sufferings. Smith believes him, feels intense pity, and gives him money. But suppose that the beggar was deceiving Smith, that he had no wife?

(b) Jones is a timorous man, and when he hears a noise downstairs one night, he thinks it is a burglar. When his wife asks him why he doesn't go down to investigate, he says that he is afraid of the burglar. But suppose that there isn't a burglar?

(c) In *The Magic Flute*, Tamino is shown a picture of Pamina, whereupon he falls in love with her. Consider a variation on the story in which the whole thing is a hoax. The picture is not a portrait of anyone.

Let us call emotions which are based in this way on a mistaken existential belief malfounded emotions. Frequent philosophical usage would allow such emotions to be emotions with objects, for the objects of mental states and attitudes are generally said to be 'intentional'. By this is meant that they need not exist. I think that the notion of an intentional object is a dangerous one. It leads to treating malfounded emotions as on a par with well-founded emotions. I shall argue, on the other hand, that it is more enlightening to treat as central emotions directed towards items in the world. Putting well-founded emotions in the centre of the picture, giving an account of them first, and only then extending the account to deal with malfounded emotions, affords the best hope of understanding these phenomena.

If objects of emotions are internalised, if they are said to be intentional objects, which may or may not exist, then the connection of emotions to items in the world acquires an aura of mystery. It seems to become accidental, and irrelevant, that an item of the appropriate kind exists. Furthermore doubt is cast on causal accounts of object-possession. For if, so to speak, something doesn't have to exist in order to be the object of an emotion, then *ipso facto* it doesn't have to be causally related to the emotion in any way. At the very least, the causation would be forced back inside the mind itself. It might still be the case that the object of an emotion was a function of the beliefs or thoughts that caused it.

I shall have more to say on this later. I do not necessarily wish to deny that the notion of an intentional object, if used with due care, might serve a useful purpose. However, I think it is more helpful to restrict the term 'object', as I shall do, to items in the world, and to deny that malfounded emotions have objects. If the term is used in this way, it follows, of course, that all emotions need not have objects. It is true that Kenny only claims that those emotions which lack objects are parasitic upon emotions with objects. My account of these emotions could conceivably be described in this way. But I think that the dependence that Kenny is claiming is stronger than the dependence that I shall claim.

There are two questions which must be firmly distinguished one from the other. The first is the question just discussed, whether mal-founded emotions should be said to have objects. The second concerns the way in which particular malfounded emotions can be described. In our examples, is it correct to say that Smith feels pity for the beggar's wife, that Jones is afraid of the burglar, and that Tamino is in love with the girl in the picture, or do such statements have an existential implication? The questions are independent ones, for one could allow that there was a sense in which malfounded emotions had objects, but deny that they were properly describable in the way suggested, or alternatively allow that they could be described in this way, but deny that they had objects. I shall discuss the question of description later.[4]

There is another class of emotions which is worth mentioning. These are not malfounded, in that they are not based on a mistaken existential belief, but no appropriate item exists in the world. People are sometimes said to feel emotions towards fictional characters. Consider, for instance, this quotation from *Here Comes Everybody*, by Anthony Burgess:

It seems that Joyce's intention was that the reader should find Buck Mulligan more and more detestable on each appearance, but this never happens: he is always welcome because of his wit. As for the other Antinous, Blazes Boylan, he is doomed to be ridiculous from the very start of his adulterous journey to Eccles Street, and we end with pity rather than hate. If we are really anxious to find someone to dislike in *Ulysses* we should look rather in the direction of its secondary hero, Stephen Dedalus – insolvent, bumptious, full of intellectual pride and irreligious bigotry, drunk, would-be lecher, *poseur*.

One can feel emotions towards fictional characters without believing, even temporarily, that they exist. Perhaps some element of make-believe is involved, but it is not clear that this is so.

---

[4] See Chapters xvi–xviii below.

4

(2) There is a second class of emotions which according to my usage lack objects. This class might be called the class of propositional emotions, and includes emotions which relate to possible future events. Taking the example of fear, one can be afraid of a particular person or thing, in which case one's fear has an object, but one can also be afraid that something terrible is going to happen, afraid of offending someone, or afraid to tell the truth. Similarly one can be sorry that the Smiths were not at the party, or hope to see the Queen.

I do not wish to extend the use of 'object' to cover these cases. Doing so, while continuing to use 'object' in the way one did before, would seem to commit one to the introduction into one's ontology of propositions, in a fairly strong sense. For in the previous cases, 'object' could be used in two ways. First, one could say that someone's fear or anger had an object. Secondly, one could use phrases like 'the object of Smith's fear' in subject position, to refer to a particular item in the world. One could say 'The object of Smith's fear is Jones', and thereby be making an identity statement. If one wished to extend the scope of 'object' to cover propositional cases, and to use it uniformly throughout, one would be faced with a choice. One could restrict the use of 'object' to statements like 'Smith's fear has an object'. But this would mean that one could no longer talk of the object of someone's fear or wrath in those contexts where it would be natural to do so. Furthermore the phrase 'an object' would seem to be redundant, for one could substitute a predicative expression for 'has an object' without loss. Alternatively one could allow the use of 'the object of Smith's fear' in propositional cases as well. But this, as I said, would surely involve introducing propositions in a strong sense. I do not wish to say that talk of propositions is always objectionable. There are some contexts in which proposition terminology, even proposition-identity statements, are useful. But in this case we would seem to be committed to treating propositions as things to which emotions can be related just as they can be related to items in the world. The term 'The object of Smith's fear' could refer, and refer in the same way, either to a person or to a proposition. This seems to me objectionable. Would we be happy to talk of someone as fearing a proposition, just as someone might fear a person?

Some emotions which can be described in this way can also be described as concerns with events. Thus we might describe the same emotion by saying 'Smith is happy that his son has succeeded', or 'Smith is happy at his son's success'. But fear and hope do not always admit of this treatment. Some would say that fear or hope that something will be the case are not properly speaking emotions. It certainly sounds odd to say that someone who is afraid that it is going to rain, or fears that the budget will be tough this year, is feeling an emotion. One might claim that no propositional case merited the title of emotion, but this would appear to be a legislative claim – the term 'emotion' is used loosely enough to cover at least some propositional cases.

Interestingly, the term 'intentional object' has sometimes been used of propositions as well as in the case of malfounded emotions. The questions involved seem to be quite different. For one thing, the point of saying that the object was intentional in the case of a malfounded emotion was that, being intentional, it need not exist. But those who talk of propositions would say that, whether true or false, they always exist.

5

(3) There is another class of emotions to which I would want to deny objects. Some of these might be called moods, though I don't think that the mood/emotion borderline is a clearly defined one. I am thinking partly of cases like happiness, depression, despair, sadness. These may sometimes be said to have objects, but not invariably. Even when someone's happiness is in some way connected with or occasioned by a particular person, we are not always inclined to call that person the object of the happiness. I will argue later that this disinclination may be justified.

Besides the cases just mentioned, there are other emotions and feelings for which we have no short and handy labels. These are often described analogically. Thus we might say of someone that she felt as if she were walking on air, and be reporting what could properly be called an emotion. For many such emotions it would be unnatural and forced to say that they had objects. Consider an example from *The Europeans*, by Henry James.

Eugenia was a woman of sudden emotions, and now, unexpectedly, she felt one rising in her heart . . . The luminous interior, the gentle, tranquil people, the simple, serious life – the sense of these things pressed upon her with an overmastering force, and she felt herself yielding to one of the most genuine emotions she had ever known. 'I should like to stay here,' she said. 'Pray take me in.'

One could say that this emotion has an object, that its object is the total situation, but is this not rather gratuitous?

6

There is another respect in which I think that Kenny's use of the term 'object' should be qualified. We normally distinguish between the *object* of someone's emotion and his *reason* for feeling the emotion. Kenny, however, does not draw this distinction. He says, for instance, that the statement 'I was angry because he burst in without knocking' assigns an object to an emotion.[5] But surely, as we ordinarily use the term, this statement gives my reason for being angry. The object of my anger is the person with whom I am angry. Kenny says later of another sentence that it 'contains an allusion to the object of the emotion', and perhaps this is all he means here. Presumably the former sentence could be said to contain an allusion to the object of my anger if I was angry with the person who burst in without knocking. But the sentence itself does not say that this is so. It does not entail that I was angry with him rather than, say, with my secretary who allowed him to burst in without knocking.

Of course the object/reason distinction is not a clear one, nor is it exclusive. Sometimes either term might equally well be applied. Nevertheless I think that there is a valid distinction which should be respected.

[5] *AEW*, p. 71.

VII

Objects: logico-grammatical criteria

I

In the last chapter I attempted to delimit the scope of the term 'object', but I didn't provide a rationale for it. I didn't show how the notion of an object was supposed to work. The introduction of a technical term – and the general notion of an object is a technical term – demands a justification. So I must now make clear what is meant by talking in general of objects of emotions, and must show that this way of talking serves a useful purpose.

Let us look first at what Kenny says, to see if he provides a satisfactory rationale. The emphasis he places on the emotion: object relation might lead us to expect a preliminary clarification of the general notion. But he introduces the idea of an object into his discussion without explaining it, initially in connection with fear: 'In general, Descartes treats the relation of the object of fear to fear itself as being that of cause to effect.'[1] This is legitimate, as we do talk of objects of fear in ordinary speech. But Kenny proceeds to a general statement without giving a general explanation: for Descartes, an emotion 'is merely contingently connected with its object'.[2] Since we do not have a general pre-philosophical notion of an object which will serve Kenny's purposes, some explanation is surely needed. Furthermore, even if the general notion did exist in everyday speech, it would need some preliminary analysis before much weight was placed on it.

Throughout Kenny's book there are scattered remarks of a general nature which are relevant to this question. In the chapter on 'Objects' there is a slightly more extended discussion. What Kenny says concerns primarily the *language* we use to talk about the emotions rather than the emotions themselves. Such a method of approach is commonly used. I hope through a consideration of Kenny's particular suggestions to lay the foundations for a more general critique.

---

[1] *AEW*, pp. 10–11.   [2] *Ibid.* p. 12.

2

Some of Kenny's remarks suggest that the notion of the object of an emotion is supposed to derive from the notion of a grammatical object. At the beginning of the 'Objects' chapter, he says:

The sense of 'object' which I have hitherto employed and wish now to discuss is one which derives from the grammatical notion of the *object* of a transitive verb. The object of fear is *what* is feared, the object of love is *what* is loved, the object of cutting is *what* is cut, the object of heating is *what* is heated. In discussing the nature of objects we are simply discussing the logical role of the object-expressions which complete the sense of intentional and non-intentional verbs.[3]

Such earlier explication of 'object' as he gives is in explicitly grammatical terms. 'Emotions, unlike pain, have objects; we are afraid *of* things, angry *with* people, ashamed *that* we have done such-and-such.'[4] 'It is natural to understand the phrase "the object of pride" as meaning *what* one is proud *of*.'[5] There are several points to be made about this grammatical approach.

(1) It is not clear exactly how Kenny's notion of an object of emotion is supposed to derive from the grammatical notion of an object. Kenny cannot claim that in any statement which assigns an object to an emotion, the object-phrase must occur as the grammatical object of the verb, since some of his own examples belie this – for instance, 'Her behaviour made me most embarrassed'.[6] Perhaps he would claim that any such statement can be reformulated so that the object-phrase occurs as the grammatical object – the above example might be equivalent to 'I was most embarrassed by her behaviour'. Clearly he must allow as grammatical objects of verbs indirect as well as direct objects. That is, he must allow objects preceded by prepositions.

(2) But in this case the criterion will not by itself suffice to pick out from the class of all emotion-reporting statements, those which assign objects to emotions. For there are phrases occurring after an emotion-verb and a preposition which are surely not object-phrases, that is do not refer to the object of the emotion. Consider the following examples:

[3] *Ibid.* pp. 187–8.   [4] *Ibid.* p. 14.
[5] *Ibid.* p. 23.   [6] *Ibid.* p. 71.

He is afraid *for* the second time to-day.
He felt afraid *in* the garden.
He was depressed *after* drinking too much.
She was terrified *despite* Smith's presence.
He was angry *from* 5 till 6.

If 'her behaviour' counts as the grammatical object in 'I was most embarrassed by her behaviour', then so will 'the garden' in 'He felt afraid in the garden'.

Furthermore, as Gosling points out, this criterion will not distinguish emotions from sensations. I may have toothache *from* eating too much chocolate.

(3) Another objection of Gosling's, that this criterion fails to yield a unique object, seems to me invalid. He says that 'there are a number of emotions which characteristically take two prepositions in the required way: gratitude has to be *to* a benefactor *for* a benefit, anger *with* someone *about* something, and so on'.[7] Kenny certainly speaks as though every emotion had a unique object, but I don't think he is compelled to do so. None of his theses depend on this being true. He can consistently allow an emotion to have a number of objects falling into different categories, merely insisting, for example, that it be non-contingently connected to each of them. Indeed, if my earlier claim about gratitude is correct, that it can be viewed either as a concern with a person or as a reaction to what the person did, a satisfactory criterion ought to show that any instance of gratitude has two objects.

(4) One might consider each emotion separately, and give a grammatical criterion for saying what its object is. Thus one might say that the object of gratitude is whoever you are grateful *to*, the object of anger is whoever you are angry *with*, and so on, until the list of emotion verbs is exhausted. One would then have a way of telling of any emotion report whether or not it assigned an object to an emotion.

This suggestion is surely unsatisfactory. Indeed, such an approach seems arbitrary and mysterious in the extreme. For even if one produced an individual criterion for each emotion, what would they have in common? Why should one say that all the criteria were criteria for the same kind of thing, namely objects of emotion? I will try to demonstrate the defects of this kind of approach by out-

[7] 'Emotion and Object', p. 488.

lining an analogous case. I might say that giapinity was a property of dogs, and explain it as follows: a spaniel is giapin if it is good-tempered, a terrier is giapin if it is irritable, a borzoi is giapin if it is more than three years old, a pekinese is giapin if it has had a litter in the last month, and so on through all the types of dogs. We would certainly have a way of telling of any dog whether or not it was giapin, but giapinity nonetheless seems to be an artificial property. There is no apparent reason why a feature of one type of dog should be classed together with one feature of a second type of dog rather than another. Or to put the point another way, someone who knew of only some types of dogs what features they had to have to be giapin would be unable to extrapolate. He could not tell what features other types of dog would have to have to be giapin. If one could only introduce the notion of an object by giving specific criteria for each emotion, then it would appear to be on a par with giapinity.

Indeed in one respect introducing the notion of giapinity like this seems superior to the suggested way of introducing the notion of an object. The former was introduced by reference to features of the dogs themselves, whereas the latter was introduced by reference, not to features of the emotions, but to features of statements about the emotions. I shall return to this point.

3

For several reasons, then, grammatical criteria will not do on their own. In the 'Objects' chapter, Kenny considers criteria for intentionality which are logical rather than grammatical. They must be combined with grammatical criteria, in that their application seems to depend on a prior identification of the object-phrase. In this chapter Kenny seems to assume that identifying the object-phrase is unproblematic, and to give criteria for distinguishing the intentional objects of mental states from the non-intentional objects of actions.

Kenny first considers object-phrases which are referring-phrases – names or descriptions. For these he suggests two criteria taken from an article by Chisholm.[8] The first is that neither the statement nor

[8] R. M. Chisholm, 'Sentences about Believing', *Proceedings of the Aristotelian Society*, LVI (1955–6).

its contradictory should entail that the object-phrase has a referent. The second is that substitutivity should fail, i.e. that one cannot necessarily substitute *salva veritate* for the object-phrase another phrase which refers to the same item.

I said in Chapter VI, 3, that I should later discuss certain problems about the interpretation of statements assigning objects to emotions. These problems concern the very logical features to which the suggested criteria appeal. I shall claim that in such statements there is an existence implication, and that substitutivity holds. I may be wrong in this, but I hope that I am not obviously wrong. Even if I am wrong, one should be able to introduce the notion of an object before determining that I am wrong, that is, before determining how 'Smith is afraid of X' and similar statements are to be interpreted.

Kenny thinks that 'these criteria as they stand are sufficient, but not necessary, conditions for intentionality'.[9] He supplements them with a criterion derived from the scholastics, again intended to distinguish intentional from non-intentional objects.

Where a non-psychological action brings about a change, the change is in the object and not, save *per accidens*, in the subject; where a psychological action brings about a change, the change is in the subject and not, save *per accidens*, in the object.[10]

Once again this is a criterion for distinguishing different types of object, and can only be applied if the object has already been identified. I do not think it is of much help in clarifying and elucidating the general notion of the object of an emotion. When does a change occur *per accidens*? Is it accidental if in my anger with someone I assault him?

Kenny wants to say that fear that there will be an explosion and fear of dying are cases of fear with an object. Here the object-phrase is not a referring-phrase. He introduces for such cases another criterion, also taken from Chisholm. This is that any non-compound sentence Q which contains a propositional clause P is intentional provided that neither Q nor not-Q imply either P or not-P. To be applicable to statements like 'Smith is afraid of dying' and 'Smith is afraid to tell the truth', this criterion must be amended slightly, for these statements do not, strictly speaking, contain a propositional clause. No doubt such an amendment can be made, though

[9] *AEW*, p. 198.   [10] *Ibid*. p. 196.

care is needed. One cannot simply equate these statements with statements which do contain a propositional sub-clause. 'Smith is afraid to tell the truth' is clearly not equivalent to 'Smith is afraid that he will tell the truth'.

Like the earlier Chisholm criteria, this presupposes a certain answer to a question about interpretation. Kenny would want to say that a statement of the form 'Smith is sorry that p' assigns an object to Smith's sorrow. But it is unclear whether or not such a statement implies that p.

4

Whether or not these criteria work is not of great moment, for the objections made above do not get to the heart of the matter. No doubt we could concoct logico-grammatical criteria which worked, that is which, if applied to any emotion-reporting statement, always told us correctly whether the statement assigned an object to the emotion, and, if it did, what object it assigned. But the fact is that no criteria of this kind can go any distance towards giving us an adequate account of the notion of the object of an emotion. Such criteria do not help to clarify the notion of an object. They do not tell us what it means to say that an emotion has an object, or what determines what the object of an emotion is. We need to go beyond the logico-grammatical criteria, and clearly we can do so. We can tell of any suggested criteria whether or not they work, and if they do not, we can modify them so that they do. To be able to do this, we must be operating in terms of some prior notion of object-possession. This prior notion is what we want to investigate. If certain logico-grammatical criteria work, we want to know why they work.

Again, different criteria were suggested for different types of statements, but what reason have we to think that they are criteria for the same thing? Why should we suppose that there is some important common feature of the situations being described by such statements? We could put the objection this way: we are given certain tests to apply to statements to tell when they assign objects to emotions; but what we want to know about is the conditions under which such statements are true. The tests can locate the relevant category for us, but they cannot tell us why the category contains what it does, or what it is that its contents have in common. General talk of objects of emotions is assumed to reflect a common feature shared by most situations in which people feel emotions. Such talk is only valid if these situations do share a common feature. The task is to say what these situations have in common, what it is by virtue of which we can say in any case where someone feels an emotion that his emotion has an object. A satisfactory answer must be about the situations themselves. If statements reporting such situations are similar, if, for example, any statement assigning an object to an emotion must possess a certain logico-grammatical property, this is indeed interesting. But it has to be explained by reference to what the statements describe. Discovery of the logico-grammatical property does not in itself help towards an analysis of the notion of an object.

To justify the general application of the notion of an object involves reflecting on the types of situation in which emotions are said to have objects, and showing what these situations have in common. It thus involves consideration of the phenomena, and not just of the language we use to talk about the phenomena. We are concerned with non-esoteric facts about the world, facts that everyone knows to be true. This is often what is involved in philosophy – reflection on the commonplace, attempts to arrange non-esoteric facts into a systematic and perhaps hitherto unperceived order.

Of course logico-grammatical criteria may sometimes be of help in philosophy, but they always demand a rationale. It must be shown that statements which possess a particular logico-grammatical feature serve a common function – that the grammatical or logical property of the statements corresponds to some property of the things or situations being talked about. The necessity for a rationale exists even when the logico-grammatical criterion works – that is, demarcates the right class of statements, or phenomena. We must know why it works.

I said that Kenny derived some of his criteria from Chisholm. Chisholm is not concerned specifically with emotions. Rather he is attempting to reformulate in a linguistic guise a thesis put forward originally by Brentano. However, he is subject to the same kind of criticism. Brentano claimed that psychical phenomena have a feature which physical phenomena lack – they are intentional, and this is the fundamental difference between the two types of phenomena. He elucidated the idea of intentionality in terms of reference to a content, or direction to an object, which, if not particularly helpful, is at least the right kind of attempt. Chisholm tries to reformulate Brentano's thesis in terms of the language we must use to talk about the mental. He says that in talking about the mental we must use statements which possess certain logical properties, whereas we can say all we want to say about the physical without using such statements. This seems to me to be a step in the wrong direction. Even if it were true, and even if Chisholm's claim were correct that therefore talk about the mental cannot be reduced to talk about the physical, the reformulation has about it an air of mystery which the original lacked. What is it about the mental as a result of which it must be described in this way? As a general principle it is objectionable to attribute a property to a thing on the grounds that a description of that thing has a particular logical characteristic, for this always leaves the important question unanswered: what is it about the thing as a result of which it must be described in this way?

It is common nowadays to approach problems in the philosophy of mind via consideration of the language we use to talk about the mind. Similarly it is common in philosophical logic to discuss questions about the interpretation of psychological statements, such as whether belief-statements are extensional or intensional, without first considering the relevant area of the philosophy of mind. It seems to me that this is to get things the wrong way round, that philosophy of mind is autonomous, and that the interpretation of psychological statements should be considered in the light of what is said about the phenomena they describe.

5

At one point Kenny outlines a test for finding the object of an emotion which differs from the criteria already considered. He does this in the specific context of 'because'-clauses which, he says, can be used sometimes to give the object, and sometimes to give the cause, of an emotion. The test is as follows:

Faced with any sentence describing the occurrence of an emotion, of the form 'A ød because *p*', we must ask whether it is a necessary condition of the truth of this sentence that A should know or believe that *p*. If so, then the sentence contains an illusion to the object of the emotion;

if not, to its cause. Thus . . . I cannot be angry because of the way a man speaks if I do not notice the way he speaks; but I may well be angry because I am hungry without realising that I am hungry.[11]

Although this test specifically concerns only 'because'-clauses, it may be possible to generalise it. Gosling takes Kenny to be offering a general test, on the grounds that if he isn't then he is no more interesting than his predecessors, but there is no indication in the text that this is how Kenny intended it. Gosling suggests that many statements of other forms which assign objects to emotions at least entail some statement containing a 'because'-clause.

Even 'he was angry with me' can be managed. It entails 'he was angry because of something I did' (on some generous interpretation of 'did'). The something is indeed not given, but we can still ask whether it is a necessary condition of the truth of the whole statement that he should believe that I did whatever it was.[12]

Gosling proceeds to show that if this is a test of an emotion's having an object, pointless depression fails the test.[13] Furthermore, cases of pointless depression are not parasitic upon cases of depression with a point, so Kenny's thesis about the scope of the emotion: object relation is refuted. However, this is not the present issue. Nor does it matter whether Kenny did in fact intend the test to be a general one. The question is whether his test gives an adequate account of object-possession.

(1) Unfortunately it is not clear that all statements assigning objects to emotions do entail statements which pass Kenny's test. Gosling cites the case of love. If I love someone there need not be some p such that the statement 'I love her because p' is true, and such that as a condition for its truth I must know or believe that p.

(2) Furthermore there may be some statements which give the cause, and not the object, of an emotion, but which satisfy Kenny's test. We may causally explain someone's anger by saying 'He is angry because he is in pain'. If this is taken causally, then it entails that he is in pain, and this in turn, I think, entails that he believes that he is in pain. Again, apropos of the emotion/sensation distinction, Kenny wants to say that 'because'-clauses always assign causes rather than objects to sensations, but if,

---

[11] *Ibid.* p. 75.   [12] Gosling, 'Emotion and Object', p. 493.

[13] Kenny had claimed that pointless depression was not objectless depression – to be depressed is for things to seem black to one, and the objects of depression are the things which seem black.

as seems plausible, one can't do logic without knowing it, 'He has a headache because he is doing logic' entails that he believes that he is doing logic.

(3) In some respects this criterion is more satisfactory than the preceding ones, for it does at least connect the object of an emotion with the beliefs of the person feeling the emotion, and this seems to be a reasonable connection. However, it does not go very far towards telling us what it means to say that an emotion has an object, or what determines what the object of a particular emotion is.

6

The position we have reached is this. We have introduced by extension from everyday speech the general term 'object of emotion' to refer to some common constituent of situations in which emotions are felt. Such a generalisation of everyday usage seems to accord with the way we habitually think about the emotions. The claim that there is a feature of emotion-situations which the general use of 'object' singles out does not give rise to immediate objections from common sense. Even Kenny's assertion that all emotions have objects, and that this is what distinguishes them from sensations, seems both comprehensible and plausible, even if on further reflection untrue. So there is some reason to think that the introduction of 'object of emotion' as a general concept merely gives form to a pre-philosophical way of thinking about the world. It sums up a cluster of ways of talking that we already possess.

But that the notion of the object of an emotion is intuitively acceptable is no more than the starting-point for an analysis. The task is to say what it is about emotion-situations by virtue of which the notion is generally applicable. What in general is singled out by talk of objects of emotions? If emotions are states of people, and their objects are items in the world, what is the link between them? What has to be the case if a particular emotion is to have as its object a particular item in the world? I have suggested in this chapter that we cannot answer these questions, or arrive at a general understanding of what it means to talk of objects of emotions, if we restrict our attention to logico-grammatical features of the statements which assign objects to emotions. How then should we proceed? In the next chapter I will contrast two methods of approach.

VIII

Objects: two methods of approach

I

It seems natural to approach the problem in the following way, partly because it is through thinking of emotions in this way that their relation to their objects presents itself as problematic. Mental reports fall into different categories. Some report something of a dispositional nature – they do not imply anything about the person's present state of consciousness. Reports of someone's beliefs seem to be of this kind, as do reports of his likes and dislikes. To say that at a certain time one person liked cheese and another person disliked cheese is not to say anything about their actual states of consciousness at that time – about their actual experiences, or thoughts, or feelings. Such statements could be true of them even if they were not conscious at that time at all – for instance, if they were asleep.

But other mental reports do seem to report something about a person's present state of consciousness. If A is in pain and B is not, the difference between them is not just a dispositional difference, but is a difference in the way they now feel. Reports that someone is now feeling an emotion (though not necessarily all reports that might be called emotion reports) seem to be of this latter kind. To say that someone is now feeling angry, or afraid, is to say something about what he is now feeling – it is not just to ascribe a disposition to him. To feel an emotion is to be in a certain phenomenal state of mind.

We can consider emotions from a merely phenomenal point of view. We can ask how they feel to the people who are in their grip. We can talk about the physical effects they have on those feeling them. Someone may be shaking with fear, or speechless with anger. But then we notice that these phenomena differ from other phenomenal states of mind such as bodily sensations, in that they are in some way concerned with or directed towards objects. So we ask what is involved in this. What do we mean when we say that an emotion has an object but a sensation does not? In what way is someone's fear or anger directed towards an object? How does the directedness come in? What determines the particular direction? That is, what is it about the emotion that determines which object it is directed towards?

If we approach the question in this way, we seem to be looking for some feature of the emotions themselves, some feature of the phenomenal states of mind. But what is this feature? If we look at classical explanations of intentionality, we find them curiously unhelpful. Thus Brentano says that

> Every mental phenomenon is characterised by what the scholastics of the Middle Ages called the intentional (and also mental) inexistence of an object, and what we could call, although in not entirely unambiguous terms, the reference to a content, a direction upon an object (by which we are not to understand a reality in this case), or an immanent objectivity. Each one includes something as object within itself, although not always in the same way.[1]

But this is not very satisfactory, for we want to ask in turn: what does it mean to say that a mental state refers to a content, or is directed upon an object? How does it do this?

Notice that Brentano allows that the object need not exist, and this seems quite natural if we approach matters in this way. When the emotion is founded on a mistaken existential belief, this seems to make no difference to the way the emotion itself is. Phenomenologically, the emotion is just the same. So if we are looking for a particular feature of the emotion, the feature still seems to be present in the malfounded cases. The directedness which we are trying to analyse still seems to be there. This leads us to conclude that the existence of an appropriate item in the world, and the relation of the emotion to this item, is not really relevant to the inquiry.

2

Rather than continue on these lines, I will suggest a different way of looking at the matter. We have been considering emotions initially from a phenomenal point of view, and then asking what

[1] F. Brentano, in R. M. Chisholm (ed.), *Realism and the Background of Phenomenology* (Glencoe, Ill., 1960), p. 50.

their intentionality or object-directedness consists in. We have taken the emotion, and tried to discover when and how it hooked on to an object. The fact that it makes no difference to the emotion whether the object exists or not tends to lead to an internalising of the object, with consequent difficulties about the relation between the internalised object and items in the outside world. Indeed the fact that emotions relate to items in the outside world at all may appear mysterious. In general, this approach involves starting from the inside and trying to work outwards, starting from the emotion itself and trying to work out to the outside world. It involves treating malfounded emotions as on a par with well-founded ones, and then trying to add the external object on.

The alternative approach, which may prove more profitable, is to start from the outside and to try to work inwards. Before we started with a person's emotion, and looked for whatever it was about it that gave it its object. Instead we could perhaps start with a person and an item in the world, and explore the relation between them. How do they have to be related for that person to feel an emotion towards that item as object? Persons and items in the world may be related in all sorts of ways. But sometimes a person and an item in the world are so related that the person has an actual present concern with that item. We can ask what has to be the case for this to be so. For example, if the item is an event, we can ask what has to be the case for the person to be reacting or responding to that event. Given that a person does have a present concern with an item in the world, we can look to see what determines the nature of that concern. Thus we can ask in what circumstances a person's concern with or response to an item in the world is an emotional concern or response. We can go on to ask what determines what kind of emotional concern or response it is. We can then ask what the particular force is of calling that item the object of the person's emotion. I shall suggest that even if an event elicits an emotional response in a person, the event cannot necessarily be called the object of the emotion.

Thus we take as our starting-point a person and an item in the world, and sketch in the relation between them. We look to see how the relation has to be for the person to feel an emotion towards the item as object. Of course not all emotions can be viewed as part of a person's concern with an item in the world. There will still be the malfounded emotions to be dealt with. But it may be easier to deal with these by a process of subtraction from the standard case of concern with an item in the world, than to start from a situation neutral as between well-founded and malfounded emotions, and to arrive at the object of an emotion by addition.

I do not claim that the second method is the only way of arriving at an adequate account of emotions and their objects. Indeed the first method ought in the end to lead to exactly the same point. Those cases in which an emotion has an object are just those cases in which someone's concern with an item in the world takes the form of feeling an emotion towards it as object, so whether we proceed by adding the object on to the emotion or narrowing the concern with an item down to an emotional one should make no difference. But I do think that by following the second line of approach we are less likely to be led astray. How the mind hooks on to the world is not essentially mysterious, at least not in the way that starting from within can make it seem.

3

Although I think that the second method of approach is more fruitful, there are several reasons why the first method is the more natural one to adopt.

(1) It is characteristic of the traditional philosophers that they approached problems in epistemology and the philosophy of mind from the first-person rather than the third-person point of view. But from the first-person point of view, of course, the situation seems just the same whether or not the object of the emotion exists. This leads one to treat those cases where there is no appropriate item in the world as on a par with those cases where there is an appropriate item. It leads one also to look at the emotion from the phenomenal point of view, and to try to discover what it is about it that gives it its directedness. If one looked at the situation from the third-person viewpoint, one would be more likely to see it as a matter of the interaction of two items, and to see malfounded emotions as in some sense aspirant cases of well-founded emotions.

(2) Philosophers have traditionally taken the person, or the mind, as their starting-point, and have attempted to classify mental states or phenomena into various types – sensations, emotions, etc. It is only later that they consider the relation of these states to things

outside. This is as true of Kenny as it is of Descartes or Hume. He begins by considering the class of feelings as a whole, and then asks what distinguishes the various kinds of feelings such as sensations, perceptions, and emotions, concluding, as we saw, that the 'most important difference between a sensation and an emotion is that emotions, unlike sensations, are essentially directed to objects'. Even if this is true, we are less likely to arrive at an adequate account of object-possession by proceeding in this way. Instead of starting with a single item, the mind, and its states, we should start with a pair of items, a person and a thing in the world, and explore the relation between them.

(3) We may be led to take the first line by the way in which we treat emotions as subjects of discourse. Thus we initially put the question in this form: What in general is meant by saying that an emotion has an object? The way the question is formulated seems to force us to look for a common feature of the emotions themselves.

Of course there is nothing wrong with treating emotions as subjects of discourse, with making statements like 'His fear was steadily increasing'. But it is important to realise that as subjects of discourse emotions are parasitic upon persons – that talking about emotions is a way of talking about the people who feel them. If we reformulated the general question so that people rather than emotions were the subject of it, we would ask: What in general is meant by saying that someone feels an emotion towards an object? This might still lead us to look for a feature of emotions, to ask what in general has to be true of someone's emotion for it to have an object, but it might equally well lead us to adopt the other approach, to start with the person and the object, and ask what in general has to be true if the person is to feel an emotion towards it.

In this connection it is interesting to compare emotions with attitudes. If we asked the comparable question of attitudes, 'What in general is meant by saying that someone has an attitude towards an object?', it could only be taken in the second way. And at a particular level the question one would naturally ask would be 'What is A's attitude to B?', and not 'What is the object of A's attitude?' That is, one would naturally start with A and B, and ask if A could be said to have an attitude towards B, and if so, what it was.

The difference is that emotions are phenomena, and can be considered apart from their objects. An attitude, on the other hand, is not phenomenal, it is not a present state of consciousness; to have a certain attitude towards someone is to have a disposition. One could not, or at any rate one could not generally, talk about how an attitude felt to the person who had it, as one can talk about how an emotion feels to the person who has it. Again, *pace* Kenny, there can be emotions without objects. It thus looks sensible to consider emotions initially without reference to their objects, and then ask what has to be added for the emotion to have an object. There cannot, on the other hand, be an attitude which is not an attitude to something.

In earlier chapters I referred frequently to the emotion: object relation. Nothing I have just said should suggest that this way of talking is illegitimate. What I am claiming is merely that the best way of arriving at an analysis of the emotion: object relation is to look at the relation of the person feeling the emotion to the object of his emotion, and that the way to look at this is to take a person and an item in the world, and ask what has to be true for the person to be emotionally concerned with the item in the world.

4

What we must ask, then, is when a person's concern with an item in the world can be called emotional. I suggested at the beginning of the chapter that when we say that someone is feeling an emotion, we are reporting something about his present state of consciousness. We do not always use emotion terms in this way. Sometimes we use them to attribute a certain disposition to a person, rather than to say something about his present mental state. Thus it can be true that A is afraid of B even if A is not now *feeling* afraid of B, or actively concerned with B in any way. It can be true, even if A is asleep. Similarly one can say that A loves or hates B without reporting something about A's present state of mind. Emotions, understood in this dispositional way, are not sharply distinguished from attitudes. When we refer to such a disposition as an emotion, rather than as an attitude, we perhaps imply that the person must be disposed to *feel* in certain ways, and not just to behave and think in certain ways.

Although emotion terms can be used in this way to attribute dispositions, my immediate concern is with their use to report a present state of a person. Thus if we say 'The thought of what might happen to him filled him with fear', or 'He felt ashamed of his awkwardness', or 'As he looked at her, his heart was filled with emotion', or 'He was intensely moved by the music', we are reporting something about how it was with him at that moment, and not just that he had a certain disposition. Indeed I think that when we talk in general terms of emotions, certainly when we talk of *feeling* emotions, we have in mind such actual states or feelings, rather than dispositions. At any rate I shall for the moment restrict my attention to these.

I suggested earlier that some emotions would naturally be considered as concerns with particular persons or things, whereas some would naturally be considered as reactions to events or actions, to what has happened or what someone has done. In the next chapter I shall initially consider them in the latter way.

IX

Emotion and object: reactions to events

I

Let us ask, then, when someone can be said to be responding or reacting to an event or action, when this response or reaction is an emotional response or reaction, what determines what kind of emotion it is, and when the event or action can properly be said to be the object of the emotional response or reaction.

To say that someone responds or reacts to an event or action is surely to say that observing, or coming to know of, or having his attention drawn to, that event or action has a certain kind of effect on him. That is, if his present state is a response or reaction to a particular happening, he must be in that state at least partly because he observed or learnt of that happening. The 'because', I would claim, is a causal 'because'. This claim, of course, is a contentious one, for it is against this kind of claim that appeals to non-contingency are made. I hope I have shown that objections on this ground are invalid. For the moment I shall assume my claim to be true, though I shall have to return to it later in the chapter. However, even if such a causal condition is necessary for someone's present state to be a response or reaction to a particular happening, I shall suggest that more is required if object-terminology is to be in place, that is, if the present state is to be properly describable as a response or reaction *to* that happening.

Responses and reactions to events can be of many kinds, and are not necessarily emotional. They may take the form, for example, of behaving in a certain way, of saying something, or having a certain thought. Thus someone's reaction to an explosion might be to throw himself to the ground, his reaction to criticism might be to defend himself, his reaction to a suggestion might be to think of what his wife would say, and so forth. But we are interested in emotional reactions and responses, so must now ask what further conditions hold when someone's reaction or response to a happening is emotional.

2

When does a response count as an emotional response? The notion of an emotion is notoriously vague. It is difficult to say anything of a general nature which will cover everything which might be called an emotion. Indeed a small and no doubt unrepresentative empirical sample suggests that no two people agree on what qualifies as an emotion. Hence it is not surprising that any interesting general claim about emotions is liable to be immediately confronted by a counter-example. In this whole area it is easier to make negative claims than positive ones, to say what an emotion is not than to say what it is. However, I shall try to say something of a general nature, with the caveat that my claims are to be understood as of the form 'Emotions typically . . .', or 'Emotions characteristically . . .', rather than of the form 'Emotions always . . .' Perhaps we could tighten up the notion of an emotion, but it does not seem necessary to do this, since, for our purposes at least, little theoretical importance would attach to such an enterprise. We are dealing with certain kinds of reactions to, or concerns with, objects, and whether all of these are properly called emotions does not much matter.

We might begin by saying that an emotional response or reaction must involve a change in the way the person feels. But what exactly is meant by this? The term 'feels' is not much clearer than the term 'emotion'. But when we refer to the way someone feels at a particular time, we clearly do not include the whole of his psychological state at that time. We distinguish what he is feeling from what he is thinking. The distinction between thought and feeling seems to be a distinction between something active and something passive. That is to say, to think is to do something, to feel is for something to happen to one. One's thought is to a certain extent within one's own control, whereas one cannot control, or at least cannot immediately control, what one feels.

We use the term 'feel' of organic sensations, and these may be involved in emotional reactions. Indeed for some emotions, such as fear or terror, there may have to be an element of organic sensation, though I do not know how one could show this to be so. The truth seems to be that there is a common total reaction which we call terror, and which always includes some element of organic sensation; whether, if the rest of the reaction occurred without the organic element, we would still call it terror, is impossible to say. It is certainly going too far to claim, as Perkins does, that there is always an element of bodily sensation in emotion.[1] If someone is moved by music, say, his response to the music surely need not involve bodily sensation.

What someone feels in a particular situation is closely connected with how the situation seems to him, how it strikes him, what particular aspects of the situation impress themselves upon him, and so on. Thus the expression of the feeling often takes the form not of an introspective report, but of a description or characterisation of the situation itself. If we refer back to the previously quoted passage from Henry James, we find that he conveys what Eugenia felt partly by describing how the situation impressed itself on her: 'The luminous interior, the gentle, tranquil people, the simple, serious life – the sense of these things pressed upon her with an overmastering force . . .' In some such cases there might be no other way of conveying the nature of the feeling – certainly no other way of conveying it so exactly. When one does attempt to describe the feeling itself, one often has recourse to metaphor or analogy. Thus one might say that a person felt as though the ground had crumbled under his feet. Again this gives us a better idea of what he felt than would a description of the feeling in non-analogical terms. Clearly the success of such a description in conveying a feeling to someone depends on his knowing what it would feel like, what one's psychological state would be, if the ground did crumble under one's feet.

Also involved in a person's state of feeling are spontaneous, undeliberated, impulses or inclinations to behave. Many emotions, especially those which can be seen as concerns with particular people or things, involve typical impulses to behave. Thus in anger, there may be an impulse to harm or injure the object in some way, in fear, an impulse to escape from the object, in pity, an impulse to help or console the object, in gratitude, an impulse to repay the object, and so on. The term 'impulse' is itself metaphorical, transferred from its primary application to the physical interaction of objects. But once again it is difficult to convey what

[1] M. Perkins, 'Emotion and Feeling', *Philosophical Review*, LXXV (1966).

is meant without use of metaphor. To feel an impulse to do something is not just to want to do something. I think that wants are dispositional, whereas feeling an impulse is an actual occurrence. Besides, one can feel an impulse to do something which one in no sense wants to do. For instance, standing on top of a cliff one might feel an impulse to throw oneself off, though it would be clearly wrong to say that one wanted to do so.

Of course when one feels an emotion one often does want, in a stronger sense, to act in a certain way. But such desires to behave count as emotional only insofar as the desired end is the immediate effect on the object, rather than some further consequence. Thus if one wanted to repay someone for something he had done for one only because, if one did not repay him, he would be unlikely to renew his assistance, this would not count as gratitude; if one desired to help someone in need only so as to get a third person's approval, this would not be pity; and so on. The desire must be had for its own sake.

The fact that such desires, to count as emotional, must be had for their own sake, and must be spontaneous and not arrived at by a process of reasoning, connects with the distinction that is sometimes drawn between emotion and reason. One cannot reason one's way to an emotion; insofar as one had reasoned one's way to something, it would not be an emotion. This helps to explain why one refers to long-term dispositions such as love or hatred as emotions rather than attitudes, for one cannot come to love someone as a result of a process of reasoning, as one can reason one's way to an attitude towards someone, such as approval. Of course one can reason one's way to a realisation that something is the case, and as a result of that feel an emotion, but that is a different matter.[2]

In cases of extreme emotion, of 'violent passions' such as rage, or terror, or grief, there may be a general effect on thought and behaviour, an inability to turn one's attention away from the cause or object of the emotion, and, in the most extreme cases, an inability to think calmly and coherently at all. If someone is grief-stricken over the death of his wife, for instance, he would tend to dwell on her death, continually to return to thinking about her, to

---

[2] I think that the supposed dichotomy between emotion and reason is a false one, and that seeing why this is so helps one to see the ultimate incoherence of utilitarianism. I shall return to this point briefly in the last chapter.

be unable to concentrate on anything else, and so on. Someone in a state of terror would find it impossible to turn his attention to a problem in formal logic. Perhaps when we talk of someone as being 'in an emotional state', we have in mind such dysfunctional elements. But it would clearly be wrong to erect such cases into a paradigm of emotion, to think of them as typical or central cases, although some kind of concentration of attention may always be involved.

I have listed some of the elements of which an emotion is commonly composed. An emotion is a complex state. How are the constituent parts linked together? An emotion may include an element of bodily sensation, but not all bodily sensations occurring at that time are part of the emotion. If someone had a toothache simultaneously with being afraid, we wouldn't say that the toothache was part of his fear. An emotion is not just a collection of co-occurring elements. That is, the various elements in an emotion are part of that emotion not simply by virtue of the fact that they occur at the same time. There must be a further link between them, some further interrelation by virtue of which they form a single whole. I think that this further interrelation is causal. That is, all the elements of an emotion form part of that emotion because they have a common causal genesis.

Compare the case of an illness. Someone who has a cold typically feels under the weather, runs a slight temperature, is inclined to sneeze, has a running or blocked-up nose, and so on. But these symptoms do not just occur concurrently. They have a common causal genesis, and it is this that makes them all part of the same cold on a particular occasion. If one of the symptoms would have been present anyway, it doesn't count as part of the cold. Similarly the various states that comprise an emotion have a common causal genesis. If we found in a particular instance of fear that someone's sensation as of butterflies in the stomach was not caused by what caused the rest of his fear, but would have occurred at that moment anyway – it was caused by a physical condition, perhaps – we would no longer say that it was part of the fear. So an emotion is a complex state whose principle of unity is causal.

If someone reacts or responds emotionally to an event or action, what the emotion is depends on the particular conjunction of features of the kinds considered above. It may also depend partly on what kind of event or action the cause of the reaction is, or, more precisely, what kind of event or action the reactor takes it to be. Thus one person's reaction to another's action can only be one of gratitude if he takes the action in some way to benefit, or to be intended to benefit, him, or someone with whose interests he is concerned. Again, another's action might cause in one a feeling of anger towards him, or it might cause in one a feeling of hatred towards him. In either case the feeling might include an impulse to harm the other in some way. There seems to be a difference, but what does it consist in? One might try inspecting the phenomenal qualities of the feelings, but I think it would be more profitable to consider the exact way one views the action concerned. In general, when one is angry with someone, one is angry with him for what he has done, whereas when one hates someone, one hates him for what he is. If a person's action causes a feeling of hatred in one, it is because the action is taken as a manifestation of his character, an indication of what he is. Exploring more generally the features which differentiate the emotions from one another would be interesting, and might not always be easy, but it is not of particular relevance in this context.

3

I have outlined some of the distinguishing features of those states of a person we call emotions. Now I wish to probe slightly more deeply into the notion of an object, restricting my attention for the moment to emotional responses or reactions to events and actions. I said at the beginning of the chapter that for an event to be the object of an emotional response, the response must be the effect of observing or learning of the event. This is a necessary condition, but I do not think that it is sufficient. That is, I think that if object-terminology is to be in place, indeed if an emotion or feeling is properly to be said to be a response *to* an event or action, more is required than the existence of a causal link. The emotion must also be in some sense relevant or appropriate to, or determined in its nature by, the event or action. I will illustrate what I mean, and in the course of doing so elaborate slightly further what I said in the last section about feelings, by considering the case of emotional response to music.

For an emotion or feeling to be a response *to* a piece of music, it is necessary, but not sufficient, that it be caused by listening to the music. Music might induce a feeling in me because of its associations. It might make me feel sad, because I had heard it played the evening before my wife died, or amused, because it reminded me of my mother-in-law's detestation of the violin. In such cases I think we would not say that the feeling was a response to the music, or that the music was the object of the feeling. For this we require that the feeling be caused by listening to the music, but in addition that the nature of the feeling, what the feeling is, should primarily be determined by features of the music itself, and not by its accidental association with something else. That is, an answer to the question, why this music should cause in the listener this kind of feeling, must refer to internal features of the music itself. In this sense the feeling is relevant or appropriate to the music.

In the case of emotional responses to music, many of the features mentioned in the previous section are absent – bodily sensation, impulses to behave, and so on. Indeed it may be a distinguishing feature of aesthetic emotions, as opposed to real life ones, that they are dissociated from behaviour. But what is left? What is the difference between someone who is moved by a piece of music and someone who isn't? Partly it is a question of involvement, of the concentration of one's attention on the music. But to say this is not sufficient. A person's attention might be concentrated on a serialist work, say, simply because the music was so difficult, and he might still not be moved by it. Being moved is a matter of the way one is involved in the music, the way one's attention is concentrated on it. As in the general distinction between thinking and feeling, part of what is at issue is the extent of one's voluntary control, the extent to which one's response is willed. Intellectual concentration is within one's control. Listening to a serialist work, concentrating but not moved, one can switch one's attention away from it without effort. If one is moved by a piece of music, on the other hand, one's response is not in the same sense voluntary. The music itself compels one's attention. Independently of one's will, it dominates one's consciousness so that one becomes, so to speak, lost in it, and abstracted from one's physical surroundings. Interruption is disturbing, even unpleasant.

As I mentioned earlier, there is a connection between what someone feels and the way things seem to him. A piece of music which moves one seems to one to have certain characteristics. The music

may cause in one an inclination to characterise it in certain ways
– as meaningful, or, more specifically, as tragic, or as poignant.
Music which moves one seems to one significant. One hears it not
just as a sequence of sounds, but as meaningful. But it strikes one
as significant also in the sense of important. What kind of feeling
the music evokes in one is in part a question of how it seems to one –
whether it seems tragic, or poignant, or happy.[3] It is in part also,
perhaps, a question of the similarity of the experience evoked by
the music to states of mind evoked by real life situations. But to
capture precisely what is involved when someone is moved by a
piece of music, or to describe the feeling evoked in him, is a task of
great difficulty.

When someone is moved by music there are two respects in which
his response is relevant to the music, in addition to being caused
by it. The first is that the nature of his response is determined by
features of the music itself, rather than by its association with something else. The second results from the connection between what
someone feels and the way things seem to him. In this case it is the
music which seems to him to have particular characteristics. It is the
music which impresses itself upon him as significant. If we consider other examples we can find both these kinds of relevance.
Suppose that someone's remark causes in me a feeling of horror. It
might do so in one of two ways. First, it might cause me to feel
horror simply because of the kind of remark it is. I am horrified that
anyone should make such a remark. Secondly, it might cause me
to feel horror because I realise what it implies. It strikes me that
his saying that must mean that something else is the case. We would
want to say only in the first case that the remark itself is the object
of my horror. In the first case the remark itself determines the
nature of my reaction in its own right, whereas in the second case
it causes horror in me only because of its implications. Again, in the
first case it is the remark, or the making of the remark, which seems
to me horrible, whereas in the second case it is the state of affairs
to which my attention is drawn by the remark. Thus the horror
is relevant to the remark in the two ways suggested. These two
kinds of relevance are clearly connected.

I suggest, then, that where emotional responses to events are
concerned, object-terminology is in place if two conditions are

[3] If we ask how such characteristics can be attributed to music a host of
problems are raised, with which I shall not attempt to deal.

satisfied. First, the emotion must be caused in the person by observing or learning of the event. Secondly, the emotion must be relevant or appropriate to the event. That is, the nature of the emotion must be determined by features of the event itself. In the next chapter I will extend this account to deal with emotions considered as concerns with persons or things, rather than as responses to events. To conclude this chapter, I will return to the contentious issue of causalism.

4

In this chapter I have talked in causal terms. I have said that if someone's state is a reaction, emotional or of another kind, to a particular event, then it must have been *caused* by his observing or learning of that event. But is this correct? Certainly it must be true that he is in his present state *because* he observed, or came to know of, or had his attention drawn to, the event in question. But must this 'because' be a causal 'because'? If it is not a causal 'because', what is it? Suppose that someone said that the reaction is connected to the event not as effect to cause, but as reaction to object, and that the 'because' is the 'because' appropriate to this relation. This will not do, for the reaction: object relation is precisely the one whose nature we are trying to analyse. I have claimed that the relation is to be understood in causal terms, and have suggested the outline of an analysis. Someone who disputes the possibility in principle of a causal account cannot base his objection *simply* on the fact that the event is the object of the reaction, for to do so would be to beg the question at issue. Furthermore, he must provide an alternative account of the relation, and of the force of the 'because' – but no such alternative account is forthcoming.[4]

Of course further grounds of objection have been adduced, notably the argument from non-contingency criticised earlier, and another general argument to be dealt with in Chapters XII and XIII. What I want to consider here is not how philosophers have argued against a causal account, but why they should have felt impelled to do so. I suggested that an emotional response to an event must be

[4] For comparable criticism of philosophers who claim that explanation in terms of reasons has no causal force, see Davidson, 'Actions, Reasons and Causes', especially pp. 690–3.

relevant or appropriate to the event. This suggestion leads naturally on to what may be one of the motives behind the anti-causal movement. It may be felt that to see the emotion: object relation in causal terms is to rule out a certain kind of assessment or appraisal of the object, or of the response to the object. Consider, for instance, the following quotations from Casey's *The Language of Criticism*:

On the one hand the work of art does not 'cause' my response. I justify my attitude, I give reasons.[5]

I am not sure that this commits [Mrs Langer] to a *causal* account, but she is certainly not leaving room for the giving of reasons – for justification.[6]

If we talk of works of art as 'arousing' or 'evoking' emotions, and if in so doing we use causal language – which is almost inseparable from 'affective' theories – we fall into a major difficulty. How do we say *what* emotion a work of art does, or should, arouse?[7]

What is required is a justification of our response. The play is the object not the cause of our response, and what we justify is an attitude.[8]

Casey seems to think that talk of the object, the work of art, say, as causing the emotional response rules out the possibility of justifying the response, or of assessing its appropriateness to the work of art in question. This may be because he feels that an emotion *caused* by a work of art would be on a par with an emotion caused by a drug, and that no more could be said about the former than about the latter. He may feel that if the emotional response is caused by the object, the person cannot help but respond in that way. How then could his response be said to be inappropriate?

However, the fact that a response of any kind is causally determined by the situation which elicits it in no way invalidates assessment of it in terms of appropriateness. Consider first a non-emotional response. Suppose we ask whether or not a creature's behaviour in a particular situation is appropriate. The criteria of appropriateness will be determined by the creature's ends of action. As an approximation, the behaviour will be appropriate to the situation if behaving in that way in that situation is likely to achieve the creature's ends. That the behaviour is caused by the creature's per-

[5] p. 8.　　　　[6] p. 82.　　　　[7] pp. 89–90.　　　　[8] p. 90.

ception of the situation does not exclude the application of these criteria of appropriateness. On the contrary, the criteria of appropriateness for behaviour *in this situation* can only properly be applied if the creature is truly behaving *in this situation,* that is, if the creature's behaviour *is* causally affected by its perception of the situation. There may be a sense in which the creature could not have behaved other than it did. But this does not alter the fact that its behaviour is or is not appropriate to the situation, i.e. that it is or is not likely to achieve the creature's ends.

Where emotional responses to objects are concerned, the criteria of appropriateness may sometimes be partly determined by reference to the responder's ends. Thus fear of an object is reasonable or appropriate if the object is likely to harm the responder in some way. Of course in the case of most emotions, the criteria of appropriateness are not wholly determined by reference to ends, and in the case of responses to works of art, perhaps not at all. Nevertheless, whether the criteria can be applied does not depend on the response being causally undetermined. Criteria of appropriateness might seem out of place if a particular work of art *always* caused a particular response – if it were a Pavlovian matter of stimulus and response. Although the perception of the work is the cause, strictly speaking, of the response, *what* effect it produces depends in part on the nature of the responder, and this in turn depends on innumerable other factors concerning his past experience, genetic make-up, etc. So different people will respond to the same work in different ways, and the same person will respond in different ways at different times. Here is one difference between an emotion produced by a work of art and an emotion produced by a drug. A drug produces an invariant effect, so there is no room for saying that one effect is more appropriate than another.

In short, there is a sense in which, even though the work of art caused the response, it could have caused a different response, and thus there is room for assessment of the response as appropriate or inappropriate. Perhaps there is another sense in which, given the stimulus, and given the responder's total present state, he could not have responded other than he did. In this sense, nothing could have happened other than it did. The application of criteria of appropriateness is not thereby ruled out. But a more general threat to any talk of justification may be felt, for here looms the problem of free will. This is a general problem, a problem of reconciling the evaluation and justification of human action with a view of man as part of a causal order. It is not specific to emotional responses to objects, and cannot be solved by denying that the emotion: object relation in particular is a causal one.

X

Emotion and object: the general conditions

I

In the last chapter I suggested that an event could be called the object of an emotional response if the response was caused by observing or learning of the event, and if the response was in addition relevant or appropriate to the event in a way I tried to describe. In this chapter I will extend the discussion to objects of emotions which are not events. I will then, in the next chapter, return to some earlier questions which were left unanswered.

Let us consider emotional concerns with persons. What has to be true for one person, *B*, to be the object of an emotion felt by another person, *A*? First, it must surely be the case that *A*'s emotion is caused by perceiving *B* or by thinking about *B* or by in some way having his attention drawn to *B*. Let us put this generally by saying that *A*'s emotion must be caused by attending to *B*. But more is required if *A* is to feel an emotion towards *B* as object. Just as in the musical example, sight of *B* might cause *A* to remember and feel an emotion about some other person. *A*'s emotion will only have *B* as its object if it is relevant to *B* in some way further to being caused by attention to *B*. The nature of *A*'s emotion must be determined by features of *B* himself, or perhaps better, by features which *A* attributes to *B* himself.

Emotional concerns with persons typically, and perhaps necessarily, involve impulses or desires to behave. The relevance of an emotion to its object manifests itself in behaviour towards the object. That is to say, *A*'s anger with *B* consists in part in an impulse or desire to harm *B*, his pity for *B* consists in part in an impulse or desire to help *B*, his gratitude to *B* consists in part in an impulse or desire to repay *B*, and so on.

It is only when this further relevance is present that object-terminology is in place. I mentioned in Chapter vi, 5, that there are emotions like happiness where, even if *A*'s happiness is caused by something which concerns *B*, we might still be reluctant to say that *B* is the object of *A*'s happiness. For example, if *A* is happy because *B* has met his just deserts, it would be odd to call *B* the object of *A*'s happiness. We can see now why this should be so. Even if being happy affects *A*'s behaviour or behavioural tendencies, it need not do so in any specific way, that is, in any way particularly relevant to the person whose downfall caused *A*'s happiness. In general those feelings like happiness and despair, which have an undifferentiated effect on behaviour, are those to which object-terminology is commonly inappropriate.

Generally, if an emotion or feeling is to have a particular item as its object, it must be caused by what we can call, to use the most comprehensive term available, attention to that item – perceiving the item, or thinking about it, or having one's attention drawn to it, or learning something about it, or, in the case of events or actions, coming to know that it occurred. But this is not sufficient for the item to be the object of the emotion. The reaction or response, the present state produced, must be in some further sense relevant to the item. It must not just be caused by attention to the item, but must be more specifically determined in its nature by the item.

There are in fact two aspects to this. The first is that what kind of emotion is felt should be determined primarily by features of the item itself, or features attributed to the item itself, rather than by the accidental association of the item with something else. The second is that the emotion should be specific to the item in a sense which I will attempt to clarify by contrast with the eye-blink reaction. Any fast-moving object approaching the eye will cause blinking, but this reaction is invariable. One case of blinking differs from another only in its cause. The reaction does not vary systematically with the object that induces blinking. When an object arouses fear, on the other hand, the response is specific to the object. Thus if there are behavioural tendencies involved, these relate to the particular object in question – when perception of *A* causes fear, the behavioural impulse involved is, let us suppose, to escape from *A*, when perception of *B* causes fear, it is to escape from *B*, and so on.

Thus typically an emotion will have a twofold relevance to its object. First, it will be caused by the apprehension of certain characteristics in the object, and will be specific and appropriate to those characteristics. Secondly, it will involve certain tendencies or impulses to behave specifically with regard to the object. To take an example, pity for someone must be caused by the apprehension of him as unfortunate, and must include an impulse to help him. As this example suggests, the same features of an emotion may determine what kind of emotion it is and to what object it is directed. That is, those features of a person's emotion by virtue of which it is pity are the features by virtue of which it is pity for a particular object.

I have attempted to indicate how the relation between a person and an item in the world has to be for the person to have an emotional concern with that item, and for talk of the object of the emotion to be in place. Not all emotions figure in the appropriate way in the interaction between persons and items in the world, and therefore to not all emotions can objects properly be attributed. The emotion: object relation has to be understood in causal terms, for the interaction between persons and the world wherein objects elicit emotions is a causal interaction. In this way the relation between an emotion and its object is not at all mysterious, but reduces to a familiar and comprehensible one. But to say that an item is the object of an emotion is not just to say that it is its cause. The notion of an object is a more specific notion.

Although the general use of the term 'object' may be technical, it is justified by common features of the phenomena. Many, though not all, emotions do share a common feature, that is, they play a common part in the interaction between men and the world. It is by reference to this that the grammatical criteria appealed to by Kenny can be seen to form a cluster. They cannot by themselves be used to define the notion of an object. But if an account of the notion is independently given, we can see why the different grammatical usages seem to belong together. For they all serve as ways of attributing objects to emotions.

My account has been in general terms, and many details remain to be filled in. Much more could be said about the precise circumstances in which talk of objects is legitimate, and about the way in which the general notion of an object can be made specific for each emotion. Such further elaboration would be of only limited interest. The same cannot be said, however, of two objections which might be made to my account. I will raise these at the end of the next chapter.

2

I said in the last section that emotions typically arise from the apprehension of certain characteristics in the object, and include certain tendencies or impulses to behave with regard to the object. That we have a use for emotion-words like 'pity', 'envy' or 'fear' rests on the existence of such regular concatenations of perception and response. Pity for someone is caused by the perception of him as unfortunate, and includes the impulse to help him. But that such a perception typically elicits such a response is by no means logically necessary. It is a contingent fact about human beings that they feel pity. There may indeed be societies where no such emotion exists. Conceivably in some society the perception of misfortune typically causes the impulse to mock. Such a society would not possess the concept of pity. It is contingent that a certain type of situation characteristically produces a certain type of response, but on such contingencies rest the possession and utility of our emotion-concepts.

The existence of some characteristic responses to similar situations may be culturally determined. The stock of common emotions may vary from society to society. But there will be a constant sub-set whose roots are biological. This will include, in particular, those emotions we share with animals.

Philosophers generally consider emotion in human terms. But a limited range of emotion words are applied to animals, and such application is not always sentimental anthropomorphism. The emotion most commonly attributed to animals is fear. Here is a quotation from a psychologist:

The stimuli that elicit fear increase in number and complexity as we go up the evolutionary scale. Donald Hebb gives the following examples: A rat is made fearful by pain, sudden loud noise, sudden loss of support, and strange surroundings. A dog is also made fearful by these things but, in addition, may be frightened by a balloon being blown up, its master in unusual clothing, or a strange person. Monkeys and apes are made fearful by an enormous list of things. . .[1]

Although in many of these cases it would be appropriate to say that the animal's fear has an object, this is not always so. Take the

[1] E. J. Murray, *Motivation and Emotion* (Englewood Cliffs, N.J., 1964), pp. 51–2.

example of a rat made fearful by a sudden lack of support. We would not want to say that the rat was afraid of the sudden lack of support. We would say that although the fear has a cause, it does not have an object. Although behavioural tendencies are involved, they are not concerned with any particular thing. There is no particular thing from which the rat will try to escape. The rat's fear has an undifferentiated effect on its behaviour.

When Kenny said that fear without an object was parasitic upon fear of an object, he did not consider such cases. The fact that undirected fear of this kind seems to be more frequent the further we go down the evolutionary scale might lead us to suppose that it couldn't be shown to be parasitic upon fear of an object. On the other hand, it may be that this state of the rat only qualifies as fear because it is relevantly similar to states commonly induced in a rat by perception of a particular object, and causing it to try to escape from that particular object. Perhaps this is so however simple an organism we consider. In other words, perhaps we can only attribute fear to those organisms of which we can sometimes say that they are trying to escape from a particular thing.

We can attribute fear to animals, and one or two other emotions such as rage. Most emotions, however, we cannot attribute to them. Most emotions involve beliefs and desires which can only be had by a user of language.[2]

3

That we possess a common stock of emotional responses helps to explain how we can understand one another. In any society the emotions provide a characteristic medium through which perception of the world is translated into action. They are shared responses to situations, whose roots are partly cultural, partly biological. They result not just in common patterns of action, but also in common ways of perceiving the situations in which action takes place. Someone will attach significance and importance to those events and to those attributes of the people around him for which he possesses characteristic responses. One man will tend to see another's misfortune as an important fact about him to the extent that he has a typical response to misfortune.

[2] On this kind of issue, see J. F. Bennett, *Rationality* (London, 1964).

Because emotions are common, they are also comprehensible. That members of a society respond similarly to similar situations renders their behaviour mutually intelligible. Another man's behaviour makes sense to me if it springs from a feeling which forms part of my own set of characteristic responses. If I know how it feels to feel as he does, I can understand how he defines the situation in which he is acting, and why he acts as he does. If the feeling out of which his action springs is foreign to me, to that extent his action is unintelligible. If someone acts out of pity, I can only understand what he does if I know what it is like to feel pity.

In so far as emotions are culturally determined, and specific to particular societies, it will be difficult for members of different societies to understand one another. I would reject, however, the extreme cultural relativism embraced by some philosophers. One can understand a way of responding that one does not share, for one can enter imaginatively into another's experience. But one can do so only on the basis of considerable knowledge of the society in question, and of the modes of thought prevalent in the society.[3] For particular emotions are not isolated ways of responding. They form part of a larger pattern, which is common to a society. A feeling such as pity, or gratitude, makes sense only in the context of a general view of man, of his relationship to other men and to the world around him, and of the framework of mutual obligations and expectations within which social life proceeds.

Emotions gain their sense from this larger context; they also provide a medium through which such general views are manifested. That is, how someone generally conceives of himself and of his fellow men is shown in his specific responses to the specific situations that confront him. How a man perceives racial differences is better indicated by his feelings when a coloured family moves in next door, or when his son decides to marry one of them, than by what he says or even thinks in abstraction from such concrete situations. Emotions are the final touchstone of sincerity.

In these ways emotions are central to human interaction. Through them how people act in the world and towards one another is made comprehensible. That the dimension of feeling is in this way central

[3] The role of literature as a means to imaginative insight should be mentioned. A more adequate treatment of the themes touched on here would take account of variations within as well as between societies.

can be brought to bear on the question raised at the beginning of the book, what marks off man from the world around him? It would be possible to construct in a machine analogues of human thought and action. But could one construct in a machine an analogue of feeling? And in the absence of this, would the behaviour of a machine ever be comprehensible in the way that human behaviour is comprehensible? I shall take up this point again in the last chapter.

XI

Emotion and object: some residual problems

In this chapter I will tie up some of the loose ends that have been left dangling from earlier chapters. I will deal first with malfounded emotions, emotions which seem to have an object, but for which no appropriate item exists in the world.

There is a class of relations which might be called template relations. If a template T fits round an object O, the hole in T must be a certain shape and size. What shape and size it must be varies with the particular object O. These characteristics of T can be specified with reference to O, for the hole in T must be the same shape and size as O. But in any case they can also be specified without explicit reference to O. Thus the hole in T might have to be circular, and of diameter fifty millimetres. As a corollary to this, we can tell just from looking at T what kind of object it does fit round. We can tell what kind of object it would fit round, even if no such object exists. We can tell, that is, just from an examination of T itself, that it would fit round a circular object of diameter fifty millimetres, without looking to see if there is an appropriate item in the world. The hole in T can only be filled in a certain way.

In general a relation R is a template relation if for A to have relation R to B, A must possess certain characteristics which vary with B, which can be specified with reference to B, but which can also be specified without explicit reference to B. From the nature of A itself one can tell to what kind of item A can have the relation R, in advance of knowing whether there is in fact anything to which A has this relation. In this sense, similarity is a template relation, but proximity is not.

The relation of emotion to object is a template relation. If someone's subjective state is an emotion felt towards B as object, it must possess certain characteristics which can be specified by reference to

B, but which can also, at least in principle, be specified without explicit reference to B. Thus, oversimplifying greatly, let us suppose that for A's state to be anger with B, it must be caused by learning something about B, and must include an impulse to harm B. It would be possible in principle to refer to the same characteristics of A's state without explicit reference to B. A's state must be caused by coming to believe that a person satisfying a certain description has done something, and must include an impulse to harm anyone he takes to satisfy that description. Again, conversely, just from the nature of A's subjective state we can tell what description the object of his anger must satisfy. We might say, metaphorically, that once again there is a hole which can only be filled in a certain way.

Through human fallibility, a person sometimes comes to believe that an object of a certain kind exists when no such object exists, or that an event of a certain kind has occurred when no such event has occurred, and such an acquisition of belief may cause in him an emotion which, were there an object or event of the kind in question, would be appropriate to it in the requisite way. Thus, to take the examples given in Chapter VI, 3, Smith's feeling of pity is caused by being told that the beggar has a wife, and how she is suffering, and includes an impulse to help anyone he took to be the beggar's wife, Jones' feeling of fear is caused by his taking a noise to be made by a burglar, and includes a disinclination to go downstairs where he thinks the burglar is, and so on. As explained above, although no item of an appropriate kind exists, the nature of the person's subjective state determines what description an item would have to satisfy to be the object of his emotion. Thus in the case of Smith, the item would have to be a woman married to the beggar, in the case of Jones, it would have to be a burglar causing the noise Jones heard, and so on. The emotion, although having no object, because no item of the right kind exists in the world, yet seems to be directed towards an object.

Indeed, as I said earlier, from the point of view of the person feeling the emotion, the situation seems to be exactly the same whether or not an appropriate item exists in the world, and this is what tempts philosophers to talk of intentional objects, objects which don't have to exist. However, as I have explained, I prefer to say that these malfounded emotions have no objects. They are similar to emotions with objects in that all the subjective conditions for object-possession are satisfied; they are defective in that no appropriate item exists in the world. Viewing matters in this way, we see malfounded emotions as aspirant cases of emotions with objects. We understand them by subtraction from the central cases of emotions directed towards objects, as satisfying some of the requirements for possession of an object, but lacking the crucial relation to an item in the world.

2

In the light of the last section, I would like to return briefly to certain points concerning the description and identification of emotions. I said in Chapter III, 4, that it was reasonable to suppose that if two items are causally connected, one must be able to give a description of either without reference to the other, a description, moreover, which could enter into a causal law. I also said that if this condition was not satisfied, doubt would be cast on the *distinctness* of the items being described. It should now be apparent that an emotion can be described in the relevant way without reference to its object, for it can be described in terms of the *kind* of item anything which was its object would have to be. If I describe an emotion in terms of the *kind* of item anything which was its object would have to be, I am not thereby referring to its object, any more than in describing a template in terms of the kind of thing it would fit round, I am referring to any particular thing it would fit round.

Much the same can be said about the identification of emotions. In Chapter V, 3, I consider a possible argument which depended on the premiss that an identifying description of an emotion, that is, a description which picks out at most one item, must refer to the object of the emotion. We now see that this premiss is false. There is a way of giving an identifying description of an emotion which does not refer to its object, namely by describing it in terms of the kind of item anything which was its object would have to be. Note that when I say that an emotion could be described in this way, we could spell out the description without the use of object-terminology. That is, we could describe the emotion in terms of the features which determine what kind of item its object would have to be – the behavioural impulses involved, and so on.

I said in the same section of Chapter V, that in attributing an object to an emotion, one seemed to imply something about the emotion's present nature, and not to be talking solely about its causal history. This has been borne out by the account given, for if an emotion has as object a particular item, it must not just be caused by attention to that item, but must have some further relevance to it, in a sense which I tried to indicate. In this way, to say that two states of fear have different objects is to say more than that they differ in their causal genesis.

I went on to mention the difference between emotions and sensations. Kenny claimed that the fact that emotions have objects, and sensations do not, is an important difference between them. Why do we not say that pains have objects? One reason is that pains are not generally caused by attention to items. That is, if an item in the world elicits pain in a person, the causation is not normally mediated through the person's perceptions and beliefs, in the way that it is when an item elicits an emotion. One can, I suppose, imagine a counter-example. I might be caused pain by hearing a very loud sound. In this case I might also have a behavioural impulse with regard to the sound, to turn it off, or to blot it out in some way. We still would not say that the sound is the *object* of the pain. This is because we do not refer to the total reaction to the sound as pain, but only to a particular element in that reaction. That is, the pain does not include the behavioural impulse, but they both form part of a total reaction, which we might call distress. We could quite reasonably say that the sound was the object of the distress. In this way the sensation of pain would bear much the same relation to the total reaction of distress as the bodily sensations involved in fear bear to the fear.

Pain itself does not vary systematically with the cause of pain. Like emotions, sensations differ from one another in being differently caused. But unlike emotions, they do not have the kind of further relevance to items figuring in their causal histories which lies behind our talk of objects of emotions. That emotions have objects and sensations do not is an important difference between them, but it is not, as Kenny's treatment seemed to suggest, an isolated difference. It results from and is bound up with all sorts of other differences.[1]

[1] Hunger seemed to be a stumbling-block for Kenny, but it is surely a mistake to view hunger as a kind of sensation. Rather it is a desire or need. Of course there are sensations of hunger, but these are to be understood as the kind of sensations one typically has when one is hungry, that is, when one has a need for food.

3

Kenny's second pattern of argument, which I discussed in Chapter v, 2, depended on the premiss that there are restrictions on the kinds of objects that the various emotions can take. Even though the argument is invalid, the premiss deserves separate consideration. Kenny says that on Hume's view of emotions,

It always happens that we feel proud of our own achievements and not, say, of the industry of ants in stone-age Papua; but the suggestion that we might feel proud of such things is as perfectly intelligible as the suggestion that the trees might flourish in December and decay in June.[2]

Clearly he sees this as a defect in Hume's theory, and wants to say that this suggestion is not intelligible. Later he says that 'In fact, each of the emotions is appropriate – logically, and not just morally appropriate – only to certain restricted objects. One cannot be afraid of just anything, nor happy about anything whatsoever.'[3]

I think that there is a point here, but that Kenny's formulation of it is slightly misleading. If I am to feel proud of an item, I must take that item as in some way connected to myself. But this is not a restriction on the object. It is a restriction on my view of the object, on the way I take the object. There are no items of which I could not feel proud, given suitable circumstances. Thus if I thought that I was the god particularly responsible for ants, I might well feel proud of the industry of ants in stone-age Papua. Perhaps for some emotions and for some items I couldn't be *that* mistaken, and still be concerned with *that* item, but this does not seem to be so with pride.

Kenny half-sees this point, but is handicapped by his determination to fit everything into a scholastic framework:

What is not possible is to envy something which one believes to belong to oneself, or to feel remorse for something in which one believes one had no part.

The medieval schoolmen gave expression to restrictions such as those we have outlined by saying that the formal object of fear was a future evil, of envy another's good, of remorse one's own past sins . . . It is not, of course, correct to say e.g. that the formal object of envy is another's good *tout court*: one must say that it is something *believed to* be good

[2] *AEW*, p. 24.   [3] *Ibid*. p. 192.

and *believed to* belong to another, as our example above shows ... The description of the formal object of a mental attitude such as an emotion, unlike a description of the formal object of a non-intentional action, must contain reference to belief. Only what is wet in fact can be dried, but something which is merely believed to be an insult may provoke anger.[4]

To say that only what is wet can be dried is, I suppose, to impose a restriction on the possible objects of drying. But whereas to say that one can envy only what belongs to another is to restrict the objects of envy, to say that one can envy only what one believes to belong to another is to restrict not the objects of envy but the envier's beliefs.

In fact, this is to put the matter the wrong way round. It is not so much that the emotion restricts the object, or the beliefs about the object. Rather it is that the object, or the beliefs about the object, restricts the emotion. That is, what emotion I can feel towards an item in the world is restricted by what I take to be true of that item. It is necessary to repeat that even if this restriction is logical, even if it is not logically possible for me to be proud of something if I do not take it to be in some way connected to myself, this in no way shows the impropriety of talking in causal terms.

4

I have tried to outline the conditions under which a person feels an emotion towards an item in the world as object. One condition is that the person should feel the emotion as a result of attending to the item. The route from object to emotion runs through the person's perceptions and thoughts. We can divide it into two stages, the first from the object to attention to the object, the second from attention to the object to the emotion. A possible objection to my account arises in connection with each stage.

(1) Is it legitimate to explain the emotion: object relation in terms of what I called generally attention to an item, that is perceiving or thinking about or having one's attention drawn to an item? An objector might feel dissatisfied with my account, for he might feel that such mental states share the very feature of emotions which the account purports to explain. Anyone who was puzzled about the

[4] *Ibid.* pp. 193–4.

relation of emotion to object might be equally puzzled about the relation of perception or thought to object. He might argue that my account left all the important questions unanswered, for there is a general problem concerning the relation of the mind to the world. Explaining the relation of emotion to object in terms of the mental state by which the emotion is caused merely pushes the problem a stage further back. I shall consider this objection in Chapter xiv.

(2) I claim that the emotion is *caused* by a mental state, namely attention to the object. That is, the analysis of the emotion: object relation involves a species of mental causation. Now there is a pattern of argument which some philosophers have used to show either that causal notions cannot be applied to the mental sphere, or that in this sphere a particular kind of causation prevails, distinct from that prevalent in the physical sphere, and not to be analysed in Humean terms. This pattern of argument relies not at all on the notion of non-contingency. I shall consider it in the next two chapters, approaching it initially as applied to the emotion: object relation.

XII

Immediacy and incorrigibility

I

I said in Chapter II, 3, that one must distinguish the question of the basis on which a claim is made from the question of the nature of the claim itself. But each of these questions can be further subdivided. As regards the basis of a claim, one can ask whether a claim is based on the explicit consideration of evidence. Some claims are so based. Perhaps what has happened in similar situations in the past is consciously considered. Other claims are immediate. They are not based on assessment of and inference from evidence. It is plausible to say that claims about the position or movement of one's own limbs are usually immediate in this sense. Miss Anscombe gives this kind of knowledge as an example of knowledge without observation.[1] She argues that when I claim, say, that my arm is straight, I do not infer that my arm is straight from any evidence. In particular I do not infer it, as might be supposed, from the sensations in my arm. Knowledge of my own future actions is also sometimes given as an example of knowledge without observation. I can say what I am going to do without having to consider how I have behaved in similar situations in the past.

Many undeniably causal claims are not based on the conscious consideration of evidence. For instance, if I drop a vase on the floor, and it shatters, I may claim immediately that it was my dropping it on the floor that caused it to shatter, without considering what has happened in similar cases in the past.

However, even if a claim has no explicit basis, it may still have an implicit basis. That is, if I ask someone who has made a claim not consciously based on evidence, 'How do you know?', he may reply by adducing evidence. He may refer to information available to him when he made the claim. Even if he did not have this information consciously in mind when he made the claim, there is

[1] G. E. M. Anscombe, *Intention* (Oxford, 1957), p. 13.

still a sense in which the claim was based on information. Had he not had the information, he could not have made the claim. Thus if I were asked how I knew that it was my dropping the vase on the floor that caused it to shatter, I would refer to information available to me, though not consciously considered by me, when I made the claim. I might mention my knowledge of what the vase was made of, and of the brittleness of this material, my knowledge of what generally causes things to break, and so on, and would say that I knew all this because of what I had observed or been told in the past. If I were asked how I knew that my arm was straight, on the other hand, I might have to reply that I just knew. There was no information available to me when I made the claim on which it was even implicitly based.

The question of the nature of a certain claim, of what is being claimed or what the claim amounts to, is different from the question of the basis of the claim. It is a matter primarily of the kind of evidence to which the claim is answerable, the kind of evidence to which appeal would be made if the claim were challenged. Now clearly a claim can be answerable to evidence even though it is not based on evidence. For instance, even if my claim that my arm is straight is not based on evidence, there are still ways in which it could be checked. If someone doubted it, he could look and see whether my arm was straight, and if necessary could compare it with a ruler or some object admitted to be straight.

What counts in assessing whether a claim is causal is the kind of evidence to which it is answerable, not the kind of evidence, if any, on which it is based. If it is causal in a Humean sense, then it is answerable to what happens in other relevantly similar situations. But as we have seen, it need not be consciously based on such evidence. Furthermore, it need not even be implicitly based on such evidence. A lucky guess can be a guess about a causal fact, though it would not, of course, count as knowledge.

A closely related question concerns corrigibility. However, this can be taken in two ways. First, one can ask whether a particular claim, say that Smith is in pain, can be shown to be wrong, irrespective of who, if anyone, makes the claim. If a claim is answerable to evidence, it must surely in principle be corrigible in the light of the evidence. It must be possible for the evidence to conflict with the claim, and thus to show, or at least strongly to suggest, that the claim is mistaken.

But secondly, one can ask whether a particular person can sincerely make the claim in question, and be mistaken. For instance, could Smith claim to be in pain, and be genuinely wrong? Certainly the claim that Smith is in pain can be checked against evidence – the cause of his sensation, what kind of behaviour it induces, and so on. Furthermore, Smith could say 'I am in pain', and the evidence could show, or strongly suggest, that he was not in pain. But it is arguable that in so far as the evidence suggested that he wasn't in pain, it also suggested that in saying 'I am in pain' he was intending to say something false, or made a slip of the tongue, or was not using the words in their correct meanings – in short, that he was not sincerely claiming to be in pain. Conversely if he sincerely claimed to be in pain, fully understanding what he said, he could not be mistaken. Whether or not this argument is correct, it shows that the question of the answerability of a claim to evidence is distinct from the question of whether a particular sincere making of the claim could be mistaken.

However, I think that for present purposes we can neglect this complication. I shall assume that in the case of the kind of claim that I shall be discussing, the fact that a particular claim, understood in its standard meaning, is mistaken, does not in any *simple* way show that the person who made the claim either was insincere, or made a slip of the tongue, or was not using the words in their standard meanings.

2

If what I said in the previous section is correct, there are defects in Kenny's own argument to show that the emotion: object relation cannot be analysed causally. He says that

If the relation between an emotion and its object were one of effect to cause, then it would be only by induction and tentative hypothesis that one knew on any particular occasion *what* one was afraid of or excited about. But this is sometimes obviously untrue. If I feel great happiness and relief because my wife unexpectedly recovers from a mortal illness, I do not first discover that I feel happy and relieved, and then draw the conclusion that this feeling is caused by my wife's recovery (e.g. on the grounds that I have observed that whenever she so recovers I have just *this* feeling).[2]

[2] *AEW*, p. 73.

But as we have seen, causal claims need not be explicitly based on induction, and certainly need not be at all tentative. A claim may be made immediately, and still be causal. A causal claim need not even be based implicitly on induction.

Kenny might reply that his point was not that I *do* not first discover that I feel happy and relieved, and then draw the conclusion that this feeling is caused by my wife's recovery, but that I *could* not proceed in this way. If the claim were a causal one, then it ought at least to be possible to arrive at it inductively. For example, take my claim that it was my dropping the vase on the floor that caused it to shatter. I could arrive at this claim by a process of inductive reasoning, even if I do not normally proceed in this way. But, Kenny might argue, I could not so arrive at the conclusion that I feel happy and relieved because of my wife's recovery.

Happiness and relief require separate treatment. In the case of relief, Kenny's claim seems to be correct, but in a way that is compatible with a causal account. The statement that I feel relief itself has certain causal implications. My feeling only counts as one of *relief* if it is caused in a certain way. Furthermore the causal facts by virtue of which my feeling counts as one of relief also establish that my feeling is one of relief at my wife's recovery – this involves no extra causal facts. It is for this reason that I couldn't first discover that I feel relieved, and then draw the conclusion that my relief is at my wife's recovery. The correctness of Kenny's claim here thus gives no grounds for saying that my wife's recovery cannot be the cause of my relief. A reformulated version of Kenny's objection would still, however, have to be met, to the effect that I couldn't arrive by inductive reasoning at the conclusion that what I feel about my wife's recovery is relief, and that therefore the statement that I feel relief at my wife's recovery cannot have causal implications. I shall return to this version later.

With happiness the case is different. The statement that someone feels happy lacks causal implications. But here surely a person might quite conceivably first discover that he was happy, and then come to some conclusion as to exactly what it was that had made him happy, perhaps even by considering how he had felt on other occasions. In this way someone might, in a particular situation, arrive for example at the disturbing conclusion that it was his wife's absence that had made him feel happy.

3

I have been considering the implication for a causal account of the immediacy of first-person assignments of objects to feelings. I shall turn now to the more direct challenge to such an account presented by the seeming incorrigibility of some such assignments. Pears considers this problem.[3] Three theses, he says, each of which individually seem plausible, cannot apparently be held together. First, many first-person assignments of objects to feelings and reactions seem to be at least partly causal. Secondly, such first-person assignments seem in many cases to be incorrigible. But thirdly, on the commonly accepted Humean view of causation, any causal or partly causal statement must be corrigible. If one of these three theses has to be discarded, which is it to be?

Pears asserts that the feelings and reactions in question lie on a spectrum, which stretches from depression at one end to amusement at the other. At the depression end, the problem doesn't arise, since first-person assignments of objects to depression can be mistaken. But at the amusement end the problem persists, since it seems that I can't be mistaken when I claim, for instance, to be amused by someone's remark.

Two, at least, of my examples are not liable to mistakes in the identification of the object, 'I was amused by his remark' and 'The explosion made me jump'. For suppose that someone tried to persuade me that the object of my amusement was really something else ... Then he would necessarily fail, because this sort of mistake is not allowed for by the concept of amusement ... Similarly, if the statement about the explosion implies that I was startled, I cannot have made a mistake in identifying it as the object of my reaction, although it may have played an unusually small part in causing it.[4]

Pears says that although such a mistaken identification is not allowed for in our present conceptual scheme, this conceptual impossibility rests on a contingent fact. There is a weak sense of 'about' in which someone is depressed about whatever he thinks about in a depressed fashion, amused about whatever he thinks about amusedly, and so on. The contingent fact underlying the conceptual impossibility is that at the amusement end of the spectrum

[3] Pears, 'Causes and Objects'. [4] *Ibid.* p. 97.

the thing which the feeling or reaction is about – in this weak
sense – is always also its cause.

If this suggestion is correct, then, though the possibility of a mistaken
identification of the object is not allowed for by the conceptual scheme at
this end of the spectrum, it still exists in the substructure of this conceptual scheme ... Though the possibility of a mistaken identification of
the object at this end of the spectrum is not contained in our conceptual
scheme, it lies only just outside it. Perhaps we could say that the
possibility of this possibility is contained in it.[5]

I shall not consider this suggestion in detail. I do not find the
distinction between a conceptual scheme and its substructure, or
between a possibility and the possibility of a possibility, completely
clear. Furthermore I think that Pears is over-concessive. I think that
none of the claims with which he is concerned is strictly speaking
incorrigible, and that no conceptual change would be necessitated by
infrequently occurring situations of the kind I shall outline, in
which such a claim would be mistaken.

The problem has not been exactly located. It is not really a specific
problem concerning the identification of objects of feelings, but a
more general problem concerning what is sometimes called mental
causation. If objects of emotions are, as I claimed, items in the
world, then assignments of objects to emotions can never be incorrigible, since existential claims are never incorrigible. For example, take the case of being amused by a remark. Pears say that
'when someone says that he is amused about a remark, he means
more than that his statement is true in the weak sense of the word
"about". He also means that the remark caused his amusement'.[6]
But the person may be mistaken in thinking that a remark was
made at all. Hence if his statement that he is amused about a remark has the force that Pears claims, it cannot be incorrigible.[7]

However, even if no first-person assignments of objects to emotions
are strictly speaking incorrigible, the problem can be restated. Pears
follows the last passage quoted with a parenthesis: 'In other cases,

---

[5] *Ibid.* pp. 108–9.   [6] *Ibid.* p. 104.

[7] Care must be exercised here, for 'remark' is ambiguous in an act-
object kind of way. A remark may be an act of remarking, or what
is remarked in an act of remarking, just as a statement may be an act
of stating, or what is stated. Only in the former sense would a remark be of the right category to be a cause.

as I pointed out earlier, it may not be the object itself but rather some thought or belief about it that causes the feeling or reaction.' A problem would arise if, even though one could be mistaken in thinking that a remark was made, one could not be mistaken in thinking that one seemed to hear a remark, or that one's seeming to hear the remark was the cause of one's amusement. Similarly, it might be claimed, even if one could somehow be deceived into thinking that an explosion occurred, one could not be mistaken in thinking that it was one's seeming to hear an explosion which made one jump.

These are examples of what Miss Anscombe calls 'mental causation'. In these cases

The cause itself *qua* cause (or perhaps one should rather say: the causation itself) is in the class of things known without observation.[8]

Mental causes are possible, not only for actions ('The martial music excites me, that is why I walk up and down') but also for feelings and even thoughts.[9]

We have given examples of mental causes of feelings, and these could be multiplied without difficulty. Examples of mental causes of thoughts are not hard to find either – perhaps I see a hippo (or seem to), and this makes me think of my mother-in-law. Once again I seem to know immediately, and incorrigibly, that it is seeing the hippo which made me think of my mother-in-law.

Miss Anscombe instructs us to

Note that this sort of causality or sense of 'causality' is so far from accommodating itself to Hume's explanations that people who believe that Hume pretty well dealt with the topic of causality would entirely leave it out of their calculations; if their attention were drawn to it they might insist that the word 'cause' was inappropriate or was quite equivocal. Or conceivably they might try to give a Humean account of the matter as far as concerned the outside observer's recognition of the cause; but hardly for the patient's.[10]

This is puzzling, since the core of the Humean view of causation concerns the *nature* of causal claims, and the kind of evidence to which they are answerable, rather than the way in which they are arrived at. The fact that claims about mental causes are arrived at *immediately* tells us, as we have seen, nothing about the nature of

[8] Anscombe, *Intention*, p. 16.   [9] *Ibid.*   [10] *Ibid.*

mental causation, and in particular does not show that it is not Humean.[11]

It is not the immediacy of the first-person claims in question that casts doubt on the ability of the Humean account to deal with these cases, but their seeming incorrigibility. How can I be mistaken in thinking that it is seeming to hear an explosion which startles me, the excitement induced by the martial music which makes me walk up and down, or seeming to see a hippo which makes me think of my mother-in-law? It may be difficult to think of an ordinary situation in which such a first-person claim would be mistaken, but I think that we can adapt a hypothetical case of Grice's to serve our purposes.

In 'The Causal Theory of Perception', Grice is concerned to show that for it to be true that X sees a clock on the shelf, it is not sufficient that it should look to X as if there is a clock on the shelf, and that there should actually be a clock on the shelf which is in X's field of view, before X's eyes, but that it is necessary that X's visual state should be causally dependent on some state of affairs involving the clock. To show this, he claims that

It is logically conceivable that there should be some method by which an expert could make it look to X as if there were a clock on the shelf on occasions when the shelf was empty: there might be some apparatus by which X's cortex could be suitably stimulated, or some technique analogous to post-hypnotic suggestion. If such treatment were applied to X on an occasion when there actually was a clock on the shelf, and if X's impressions were found to continue unchanged when the clock was removed or its position altered, then I think we should be inclined to say that X did not see the clock which was before his eyes, just because we should regard the clock as playing no part in the origination of his impression.[12]

It is surely conceivable that X's cortex could be similarly stimulated so that he showed a startle response, or walked up and down, or

---

[11] Cf. Pears, 'Causes and Objects', p. 93. Pears points out that Hume explicitly rejects the thesis that causal statements are always based on inferences in *Treatise*, 1, 3, 12 and 13. Miss Anscombe must take Hume to be concerned with the way in which causal statements are arrived at, since it is only with regard to this that a first-person and a third-person account could differ. The nature of a causal connection remains the same whatever angle it is viewed from.

[12] 'Causal Theory of Perception', p. 142.

thought of his mother-in-law. If a startle response were by such means induced in him without his knowledge (the difficulties in this are surely technical rather than logical), and if at the same time an explosion occurred, he would naturally take his startle to be caused by the explosion. Similarly it might be the case that he saw a hippo and thought of his mother-in-law, and claimed that it was seeing the hippo which made him think of his mother-in-law – perhaps he could even point out the features of the hippo which would be likely to bring his mother-in-law to mind – but that in fact his brain was so stimulated that he would have thought of his mother-in-law at that moment in any case. In such a situation we would surely say that, despite the immediacy of his causal claim, it was mistaken.

It is immaterial that Grice's suggestion may well be technically impossible. Whenever someone makes a first-person claim about mental causation, it is at least logically possible that a Gricean situation should prevail, and that his claim should be false. No such first-person claim can, therefore, be said to be strictly incorrigible. Furthermore, even if in practice many first-person claims about mental causation are immune from doubt, this is by no means universally true. People quite frequently find that they were mistaken as to what made them act or think in a particular way. Such mistakes occur in the normal course of events; they also occur, of course, in such abnormal cases as post-hypnotic suggestion.

When someone corrects his claim about mental causation, it would be over-simple to say that he does so simply by reference to similar cases in the past. But this does not distinguish mental causation from physical causation. To take the Gricean example itself, the claim that someone's startle response was caused by outside intervention in the brain rather than by an explosion would not be supported simply by reference to parallel cases. Exactly parallel cases might never previously have occurred. In general, the relation between singular causal statements and empirical regularities is, as we saw in Chapter II, a complex one. The immediate backing for a causal statement would, perhaps, be some kind of generalisation or law. This might be immediately based on empirical regularities. Alternatively, it might be derived from some theoretical system which as a whole was based on empirical regularities, even though the particular law was not. In the case of mental causation, our grounds for making a causal statement may be our knowledge of how it would be rational to behave or react in the situation in question. It would of course be a matter of empirical fact, and thus testable against empirical regularities, that people in general, and this person in particular, normally behave rationally.

I think it is clear that the possibility of the Gricean situation is allowed for by our present conceptual scheme. That is, if such cortical stimulation occurred only on isolated occasions, no conceptual change would be forced on us. Whether our present conceptual scheme could still cope if such occurrences were frequent is more dubious.

XIII

First-person privilege

I

We have shown that first-person claims about mental causation, although immediate, are not incorrigible, just as first-person claims about the position of one's limbs, although immediate, are not incorrigible. But it would be unsatisfactory to leave the matter here. First, it is a fact that seems to need explaining that such claims *can* be made immediately, that is, that one *can* make such claims without having to base them on evidence. Secondly, even if such claims are not, strictly speaking, incorrigible, they are nearly always right. This too needs explaining. But what kind of explanation should be sought?

In the cases we are considering the claim made goes beyond what is immediately available to the person making it. Thus in the case of a claim about mental causation, what is immediately given is that one mental state was followed by another. But the claim that one mental state caused or produced another is stronger than the claim that the first was followed by the second, whatever account of mental causation is accepted.[1] What we are asking in effect is how a person can make the stronger claim if he does not infer it from evidence.

In Chapter XII, I, I gave some instances of claims which were not explicitly arrived at by inference from evidence, but where one could ask how the person knew. There the reply was in terms of information available to the person at the time, information on which his claim was in some sense based, even if he did not go through a conscious process of considering it before making the claim. But this kind of reply cannot be given to the comparable question concerning non-observational claims about, say, the position or movement of one's limbs, for such claims are not even implicitly based on information available to one. Nevertheless, it is possible to give a

[1] This point is made in J. Teichmann, 'Mental Cause and Effect', *Mind*, LXX (1961).

different kind of reply to the question, a different kind of explanation of how someone knows where his limbs are. After all, it is not a miracle that we can make non-observational claims about the position or movement of our limbs. On the contrary, there must be a causal mechanism which ensures that if a person's limbs are in a certain position, or moving in a certain way, he can report where they are, or how they are moving – provided, of course, that he has the requisite linguistic capacity. We can explain the ability to make such correct non-observational claims in terms of this causal mechanism – explaining how messages are passed up the nerves, how changes are induced in the brain, and so on.

If there is a causal mechanism of this kind, one would expect that if it went wrong, it would go wrong in an explicable way. That is, one would expect that if someone was unable to make a claim, or made an incorrect claim, about the position of his limbs, this would be explicable in terms of some interference with the normal working of the mechanism, and that in the absence of such interference, his claims would be correct. This is what we find in practice. In those cases where someone does not know where his limbs are, or how they are moving, we find that the mechanism is malfunctioning – perhaps because the limb in question has been anaesthetised. But normally the mechanism functions properly, and this is sufficient explanation of our normal ability to make correct claims of this kind.

Clearly if we can make correct immediate claims about mental causation, there must be a causal mechanism of the same kind, though it may be very much more complicated. Thus a similar kind of explanation could in principle be given of our ability to make these claims. That we can make non-observational claims about mental causation and not about causation in the outside world results from the fact that no suitable mechanism exists in the latter case.

A similar explanation can be given for the seeming incorrigibility of claims about mental causation. Indeed, since the causal mechanism is contained entirely within the brain, we would expect that it would be less susceptible to disruption from outside interference. Whereas it is a comparatively simple matter to interfere with the neural connections between the arm and the brain, it is a much more difficult technical feat to intervene, at least in a controlled way, in the workings of the brain itself.

2

In a sense, then, an explanation can be given of our ability to make immediate claims of the kinds in question. It is not at all mysterious. A neurophysiologist could no doubt greatly elaborate on the matters raised in the last section. But at a philosophical level we still feel a certain dissatisfaction. For it is a mere matter of fact that a causal mechanism of the kind suggested exists, whereas it does not seem to be a mere matter of fact that we can make immediate claims of these kinds. I think that we can produce *conceptual* considerations to show that we must be able to make such claims immediately. To illustrate what I have in mind, I will deal first with the case of claims about the position and movement of parts of the body, and then move on to the more complicated case of claims about mental causation.

Intentional action can be either instrumental or non-instrumental. An action *A* is instrumental if one does *A by* doing something else, *by* performing some prior action. Thus one may move a lever by straightening one's arm. An action *A* is non-instrumental if there is no prior action such that one does *A* by performing that prior action. Thus in general if one intentionally straightens one's arm, there is no prior action such that one straightens one's arm by performing that prior action. (In exceptional cases there may be some prior action, as when one straightens one arm by holding it in the other hand and moving the other arm. But then one moves the other arm non-instrumentally.)

I think it can be shown that if one intentionally and non-instrumentally moves one's arm, then one must know non-observationally that one is doing so. Certainly one can only move one's arm intentionally if one knows that one is doing so. But further to this, I think that one can only be said to move one's arm intentionally if the movement of one's arm is in a certain sense *dependent* on one's knowledge that one is moving it, that is, if the arm wouldn't have moved had one not known that one was moving it. If the movement had occurred independently of one's knowledge, then it could not be said to be an intentional action. But if one's knowledge of the movement of one's arm were observational, if one could only tell that one's arm was moving by looking and seeing (or even from the sensations in one's arm), then one's knowledge would be dependent on the movement, rather than vice versa, and this would seem to exclude the movement from being an intentional action. If this is so, then for intentional and non-instrumental movement of one's arm, one must know non-observationally that it is moving.

Clearly if one is to act at all, one must be able to perform non-instrumental actions. That is, there must be something such that one does that not by doing anything else. Thus if this argument is correct, it is a precondition of intentional action that one have non-observational knowledge of the position and movement of one's body. Thus any agent *must* have knowledge of this kind. Of course it is a contingent fact that there are agents, and it is a contingent fact that there is anything that has knowledge of this kind. But it is not a contingent fact that if anything is an agent, it has knowledge of this kind.

I have only given the outline of an argument. To be convincing it would have to be considerably elaborated. For instance, it would be necessary to show that one does not and could not move one's body by performing some prior mental action such as voliting. I think it would be possible to show this, but it is not necessary for my present purpose, which is to indicate how the feeling of dissatisfaction remaining after a causal explanation of immediate knowledge has been given can be removed by adducing conceptual considerations.

If one has shown that an agent must have immediate knowledge of a certain kind, one can then see why his immediate claims of this kind must generally be right or explicably wrong. For this is necessary if the claims are to be knowledge claims, rather than guesses which are occasionally lucky.

3

In the previous section I suggested that the fact that agents have immediate knowledge of the position and movements of their own bodies can be given a certain kind of conceptual backing. The crucial point was that an agent must know immediately *what* he is doing. I think that a similar conceptual backing could be given for the fact that agents have immediate knowledge of mental causation, hinging on the fact that an agent must in general know immediately *why* he is doing what he is doing. But in this case I am not clear how the argument would be worked out in detail.

I think that there are two ways in which knowledge of mental causation is involved in knowledge of one's reasons for acting. First, for an agent to act in a certain way for a certain reason, he must not only act in that way, and have that reason for acting in that way, but must further act in that way *because* he has that reason for acting in that way. Davidson and Pears argue that this 'because' has a causal force. I shall assume that they are correct in this, and shall not attempt to supplement their arguments. If they are correct, then knowledge of one's reasons for acting involves knowledge of mental causation. If it could be shown that an agent's knowledge of his reasons for acting must at least sometimes be immediate, it would follow that his knowledge of mental causation must at least sometimes be immediate.

We can distinguish first-person and third-person knowledge of an agent's reasons for action. Third-person knowledge of an agent's reasons is inferential, based on information relating to this agent in particular, and information relating to human beings in general. Information relating to this agent in particular concerns his present behaviour, what his view of the present situation is likely to be and what his interests are in this situation, how he has behaved in similar situations in the past, and perhaps his own verbal reports – but these are always answerable to his non-verbal behaviour in this and other situations. But in addition we have a vast and largely unarticulated store of information concerning the forces which generally move people to act, derived from our own and other people's past behaviour, which we bring to bear on particular cases. First-person knowledge, the agent's own knowledge of his reasons for action, is generally non-inferential. He does not in general need to consider how he has acted in past situations to know why he is acting as he is. There are exceptions to this. Sometimes one can discover one's reasons for acting in a third-person kind of way. If the motivation is unconscious, this is the only way in which the agent can become aware of it.

The question at issue is whether the case in which an agent becomes aware of his reasons for acting in a third-person kind of way must necessarily be exceptional. Could there be a person who had no immediate knowledge of his own reasons for action, but had to view himself from a third-person point of view? He would of course have a much larger store of information concerning himself than anyone else would have, but in essence the situation would be the same.

I think one should be able to show that the notion of an agent who only has third-person knowledge of his reasons for action is conceptually incoherent, but I do not know how to do this. It would not be enough simply to say that the notion of an unconscious reason for action is parasitic upon the notion of a conscious reason. This may be true, but it is necessary to show it to be true. I think, furthermore, that the notions of deliberation and decision would only be applicable to someone who had non-inferential knowledge of his reasons for action, but again I am not clear how this could be satisfactorily demonstrated.

I said that there seemed to be two ways in which knowledge of mental causation is involved in knowledge of one's reasons for acting. The first way concerned one's knowledge that one acted in a certain way *because* one had a certain reason. The second way concerns one's knowledge that one has a certain reason, that is, that one has a certain set of beliefs and desires. To show that the attribution of beliefs and desires to a person has causal implications would involve an analysis of these notions, which I shall not here attempt. But briefly, I think that what someone believes and desires is at least in part a matter of how he would behave in certain situations, and that this is a matter of how his being in these situations would cause him to behave. If this is so, then knowledge of one's beliefs and desires involves knowledge of hypothetical causal facts about oneself, and thus non-inferential knowledge of one's beliefs and desires involves non-inferential knowledge of such causal facts. If it can be shown that an agent's knowledge of his own beliefs and desires cannot be only of a third-person kind, then this would be another way of showing that an agent must have non-inferential knowledge of mental causation.

Once again I am uncertain how to *demonstrate* that an agent must have non-inferential knowledge of his own beliefs and desires.[2] Certainly the idea of an agent who only knows about his own beliefs and desires in the kind of way in which he knows about other

---

[2] Given, that is, that he has knowledge of his beliefs and desires at all. It is questionable whether an animal can be said to have knowledge of its beliefs and desires.

people's beliefs and desires is a very strange one. But how can it be shown to be conceptually incoherent?

If the preceding argument falls short of proof, I hope that it has at least lent credibility to my contention that it is not a contingent fact that any agent has immediate knowledge of mental causation. If this contention is correct, then here too it is a requirement for knowledge that the agent's claims should generally be right or explicably wrong. In this way the fact that a perfectly normal kind of causation is involved in the mental sphere can be reconciled with the features of a person's knowledge of his own mind which seem to cast doubt on this. More specifically, the kind of knowledge a person has of his emotions and of their genesis is quite compatible with my account of emotions and their objects.

4

I would like finally to say slightly more about a particular aspect of knowledge of the objects of one's emotions. I said in Chapter XII, 2, that Kenny might object to the claim that the statement that I feel relief at my wife's recovery has causal implications by saying that I *couldn't* – not just that I *don't* – arrive by inductive reasoning at the conclusion that what I feel about my wife's recovery is relief.

One can generalise this question, and ask whether one must know immediately that one's reaction to an event E is F, or whether one can sometimes arrive at such a conclusion by inductive reasoning. There are in fact two aspects to this question, concerning the identification of the reaction and its description. The question of identification is the question of knowing *which* feelings, thoughts, behavioural impulses, etc., are the reaction to E. The question of description is the question of knowing what these add up to, whether the total reaction is properly describable as an F reaction.

As regards the second question, it seems quite possible that one should not know immediately how best to describe one's reaction to a particular event. One sometimes, surely, has to work out exactly what one feels. Such working out might involve gathering one's thoughts, abstracting oneself to a certain extent from the reaction, and trying to look at it as a whole, and might perhaps also involve thinking back to how one felt on other occasions. In some cases this might only be possible in retrospect. In this way, to take Kenny's case, one might at first be uncertain whether or not what one felt about one's wife's recovery was *relief*.

The first question, whether one must know immediately which feelings, thoughts, etc., comprise the reaction to the event, is more relevant to the present issue, that is, whether they can properly be said to be *caused* by the event. One possibility is this: that even though the feelings, thoughts, etc., are caused by the event, for them to be said to comprise a *reaction* to the event – and not just in some way to be indirectly caused by it – one must be immediately aware of the causation. The fact that a reaction is caused by the event to which it is a reaction is thus quite compatible with the suggestion that if it is a reaction to that event one must know immediately that it is a reaction to that event. Such immediate awareness may, indeed, be built into the logic of some of the emotion concepts (and to this extent what Pears says may be correct). For instance, I do not think that one could be said to be horrified at a catastrophe unless one was immediately aware of what one was reacting to, i.e. of what one's horror was caused by.

I am not sure, however, that the suggestion is universally correct. That is, I think that in some cases one may not be immediately aware that a particular feeling or thought is a reaction to a particular event, and may only later come to realise this.

XIV

Attention and object

I

At the end of Chapter XI I raised a possible objection to my account of emotion and object. As part of that account I said that for an emotion to be directed towards an item in the world as object, it must be caused by a mental state of a kind described as attention to the item. The objection was that my account was unhelpful, for whatever was problematic about the relation of an emotion to its object was equally problematic about the relation of such mental states to their objects. The problem had merely been pushed back a stage.

The objection should be specified more exactly. One kind of objection to an account of emotion and object would take the form of denying the correctness of the suggested conditions for a person to feel an emotion towards an item as object. Thus someone might deny that it was in general true that for a person to feel an emotion towards an item as object his emotion must be caused by attending to the item. The present objection is not of this kind. The objector does not deny that the suggested conditions really are conditions. What he claims is that to explain the emotion: object relation in terms of these conditions leaves the important problem unsolved. The feature of emotions to be explained is the way they link up to items in the world. The objector claims that my supposed explanation of this feature refers to mental states which possess precisely the same feature, and thus fails to be genuinely explanatory. The puzzle about emotions is but an aspect of a general puzzle about the relation of the mind to the world. Even if I have given a set of conditions under which an emotion relates to the world, I have done so in a way which leaves the general puzzle untouched. To give an analogy, it is as if I had explained our knowledge of the future in terms of our knowledge of general laws. Someone might say that we know that an event will occur when we know some generalisation to the effect that states of affairs of the kind presently obtaining always issue in an event of the kind in question. But what is problematic about knowledge of the future, namely the validity of inductive argument, is also problematic about knowledge of general laws, so the suggested account of knowledge of the future is fundamentally unhelpful. Similarly, the objector claims, what is problematic about emotions and their objects is also problematic about all mental states and their objects, so my suggested account is fundamentally unhelpful.

How is this objection to be met? My thesis was that if a person was emotionally concerned with an item, he had to be in a state of a kind I tried to describe, as a result of attending to that item, by which I meant perceiving the item, or thinking about the item, or having his attention drawn to the item, or whatever it might be. (I said also that further conditions were necessary, but these can be ignored at this point.) Perhaps as a first step towards meeting the objection, we should say something about the various forms of attention to an item. I shall restrict my discussion to the two central cases, namely perception of an item, and thought about an item. I shall not give a full account of these, but shall suggest what kind of account might be given in either case. I shall be interested in particular in the extent to which these relations can be called causal.

2

In the article I referred to earlier, Grice argues for a version of the causal theory of perception. He argues, in effect, that for a person to perceive an item in the world, that person must be in a certain kind of sensory state in the causal genesis of which the item figures in a certain way. I do not wish to go into the details of Grice's analysis. Whether or not his specific version of the causal theory is correct, I think that his approach is fundamentally the right one, and that when a person perceives an item in the world, the link between the item and the person's sensory state is a causal link. In this way, when a person responds emotionally to an event which he actually observes, or when the sight of a person or a thing evokes a feeling in him, there is a fairly straightforward causal chain connecting the event or person or thing to his emotion, running through his perception of that event or person or thing.

But people can feel emotions towards items beyond the bounds of their immediate sensory experience. Thinking about an event or a person or a thing can summon up an emotion. The link between an item and thought about that item is not so straightforward as the link between an item and perception of that item. What has to be true of a person and an item in the world for the person to be thinking about that item?

It is commonly said that the concept of thought is a polymorphous one. But when we use the present continuous tense 'is thinking', as in '*A* is thinking about *B*' or '*A* is thinking how to do *X*' or simply '*A* is thinking', we seem to imply some present activity, and it is with this that I am here concerned. The activity may take an overt or a covert form, but I am inclined to believe that it must involve the manipulation of symbols. That is, I believe that even in those cases where someone is thinking to himself, rather than out loud, he must still in some way be operating with symbols. So the connection between thought and the world is made symbolically.

Here we approach the edge of that philosophical jungle called 'meaning and reference', in which many explorers have perished. All sorts of difficulties are encountered by anyone who tries to state the exact conditions under which a person uses a symbol to refer to a particular item in the world. These difficulties are inherent in the very nature of symbols. The use of symbols releases thought from the confines of immediate experience, but it introduces many more ways in which the lines between the mind and the world can become tangled and blurred. There are cases where the incomplete knowledge or mistaken beliefs of the person concerned render it unclear which item he is talking about, or whether he can properly be said to be talking about an item in the world at all. To give an example, suppose that Tom says 'The man whom Mary loves is in the next room'. It might seem plausible to say that a person *A* is talking about *B* if he uses a referring phrase which, if taken to mean what he takes it to mean, is in fact true of *B*, and that thus in this case Tom must be talking about the man whom Mary loves. On closer reflection, however, this can be seen to be neither a necessary nor a sufficient condition. Tom may mistakenly think that Mary loves Dick, the local football coach, and he may make his statement because he saw Dick go into the next room. Here we would be inclined to say that Tom is not talking about the man whom Mary loves – and thus that the suggested condition is not sufficient – but rather about Dick, the local football coach, and thus that the suggested condition is not necessary. In other cases it may be quite unclear which person Tom is talking about. Suppose he says 'The man whom Mary loves is very lucky'. Is he talking about the man whom Mary in fact loves, or about Dick, or can he be said to be talking about neither?

That the notion of reference is, so to speak, fuzzy at the edges does not mean that our understanding of the central cases is unclear. I shall not tackle the general problem of meaning and reference, or of when a creature can be said to use symbols or to have a language. I shall be concerned only with the relation between particular symbols or groups of symbols and items in the world. Given that someone is using a symbol with a certain meaning, when can he be said, in using it, to be talking or thinking about a particular item in the world? I shall not attempt to produce a set of necessary and sufficient conditions that will cope with every case, for I do not think that this is needed in the present context. I shall merely try to suggest what kind of account might be given. I think that any adequate account must go beyond the bounds of philosophical logic, and in particular that it may involve the introduction of causal notions.

3

Let us introduce the notion of a dossier of descriptions.[1] A set of singular terms is a dossier for a person A if A thinks that every member of the set designates the same item in the world. Thus in the case considered above, 'The man whom Mary loves' is a member of one of Tom's dossiers, which also includes 'Dick' and 'The local football coach' and 'The man in the next room' and many other descriptions. Although the particular description that Tom used in his statement did not in fact apply to Dick, it belonged to a dossier most members of which did apply to him. It was this that inclined us to say that Tom was really talking about Dick.

Problems about reference can be raised in connection either with dossiers, or with particular referring phrases belonging to them.

[1] The notion is H. P. Grice's, who has greatly influenced my thought in this area.

One can consider a particular use of a referring phrase and ask who or what the speaker, in using that phrase, was talking about. Or one can consider a dossier independently of any particular utterance or thought, and ask who or what it is a dossier on. Conversely one can ask, of a person and an item in the world, whether the person has a dossier on that item. There are two main types of problematic case.

First, there are cases where the members of a dossier do not in fact all refer to the same item – although of course the person who possesses the dossier thinks they do. Sometimes there will be just one or two misfits in the dossier, and we will be quite happy to say that the dossier is a dossier on the item to which most of its members refer. Thus Tom's dossier in the example above is a dossier on Dick, even though one or two members of it like 'The man whom Mary loves' do not apply to Dick. Sometimes the person will have completely conflated two quite different items, so that we are not at all sure whether to say that the dossier is a dossier on one or the other of them, or on both, or on neither. Turning to particular uses of members of a dossier, problems arise when a misfit is used. We may be unsure whether to say that the person is talking about the item to which the misfit itself refers, or about the item on which the dossier to which the misfit belongs is a dossier.

The matter is further complicated by the fact that a person can sometimes point to an item in the world as the item on which one of his dossiers is a dossier. Thus Tom can recognise Dick. He can point to him as the local football coach. He will also, of course, mistakenly, point to him as the man whom Mary loves. Clearly problems arise when the man who would be pointed to is not in fact the man to whom most members of the dossier in question apply.

There is, it seems to me, a second kind of problematic case. Suppose we ask when an item figures in a person's ontology. In other words, what has to be true for a person to have a dossier on a particular item? Is it sufficient that he believe that a phrase, which in fact applies to that item, has a referent? I believe that the phrase 'The hundredth man born in Russia in 1927' has a referent, though I know nothing about the man who fits this description. Can I be said to have a dossier on this man? Again, if I use this phrase in a statement, for example if I say 'The hundredth man born in Russia in 1927 is probably still in Russia', can I be said to be talking about the man who in fact fits this description? At the least this case is very different from that in which I have a specific man in mind, who I could point to in the street, and about whose biography I am quite knowledgeable. One surely has an inclination to say that in the former case I am not really talking about or referring to a specific man, and that I do not have a dossier on the man who as a matter of fact is the hundredth man born in Russia in 1927. It is not that the dossier is so scanty. Compare the case where I pass someone in the street, and say 'The man I just passed in the street looked ill'. In this case we would be inclined to say that I had a dossier on the man in question, although a very small one.

To allow that a person has a dossier on an item if he believes that some phrase in fact referring to that item has a referent, and that he is talking about an item if he uses a phrase which applies to that item, would surely lead to paradox. We would be committed to saying in certain contexts that a person, in using a phrase, is talking about two quite different items. For in at least some cases when a person uses a phrase which is a misfit in the dossier to which it belongs, we want to say that he is talking about the item to which most members of the dossier refer. The line suggested here would mean saying that in such a case he is also talking about the different item of which the phrase used is itself true. For example, in the case considered earlier, it would mean saying both that Tom is talking about Dick, the local football coach, and that he is talking about the man whom Mary loves, who is a different man.

But worse than this, we would have to say that a dossier containing phrases which in fact referred to different items was a dossier on all those items. Thus Tom's dossier would be a dossier on Dick, but it would also be a dossier on the man whom Mary loves, and if through some further mistake it contained a phrase in fact true of some third person, it would be a dossier on that third person also. This is surely unacceptable. We want to be able to say that the dossier is a dossier only on Dick, even though one or two phrases in it apply to someone else. Similarly we need a notion of talking about such that it is not sufficient for someone to talk about an item that he use a phrase in fact true of that item.

Ordinary usage may be to a certain extent permissive. It may well be that our ordinary notion of talking about, or of reference, is insufficiently definite to give us a clear answer in these problematic cases, and that any attempt at philosophical explication will be partly legislative. But if philosophers are to legislate, if they are to turn the ordinary notion into a philosophical tool with precise application, how can they best proceed? Let us start from a case where a person has a dossier which is straightforwardly and without question a dossier on a particular item.

Suppose that a man has a dossier on his eldest son. This will include countless descriptions nearly all of which, though perhaps not quite all, in fact apply to his eldest son. In addition he can unhesitatingly pick out his eldest son as the person to whom these descriptions apply. There is no doubt that when he uses one of these descriptions he is talking about his eldest son. Now what is the link between the eldest son and his father's dossier on him? What kind of connection is there between them? It partly consists in this, that if we ask how the father came to acquire the dossier in question, his eldest son will figure prominently in the answer. The father has the dossier that he does and it contains the descriptions that it does largely because his son is as he is and has done what he has done. How the son is and has been largely determines the nature of the dossier his father has on him. In other words the son plays a particular kind of role in the causal explanation of his father's possession of the dossier. The link between the son and his father's dossier on him is at least partly a causal one.

One could construct a hypothetical situation analogous to that outlined in Chapter xii, 3. Suppose that someone's brain were stimulated in such a way that he came to believe that a certain dossier of descriptions had application. Now even if most of the descriptions did happen by chance to apply to a particular person, I think we would be reluctant to say that the man whose brain had been stimulated had a dossier on that person, or that when he used one of the descriptions he was talking about that person. The existence of a person to whom most of the descriptions apply is causally irrelevant to the man's possession of the dossier, and it is this, I suggest, that makes us reluctant to say that the dossier is a dossier on that person.

Of course very much more is involved in reference than the existence of a causal link. All I am suggesting is that looking at the causal history of the dossiers that a person possesses will help to untangle problematic cases like those considered above. Suppose we posit as a necessary condition for someone to have a dossier on a particular item that there be a certain kind of causal link between the dossier and the item. The item must be causally relevant to the dossier. How would this suggested condition bear on our problematic cases?

There doesn't seem to be any kind of causal link between the hundredth man born in Russia in 1927 and my belief that someone satisfies this description. It is not because of anything to do with that man in particular that I believe that the description has application. On the other hand if I pass someone in the street, it is because I have just passed him in the street that I have a dossier including the phrase 'The man I just passed in the street'. So our suggested condition would lead us to say in the latter case that I have a dossier on the person in question, but not in the former. Note that the causal link needn't involve my perceiving the person in question. It is sufficient that between the dossier and the person on whom it is a dossier some kind of continuous causal chain can be traced, which may, for example, be routed through the reports of others.

We can look also at the use of particular referring phrases in this light. The condition of the man I just passed in the street is a causally relevant factor in explaining why I said 'The man I just passed in the street looked ill'. Nothing about the specific man who is the hundredth man born in Russia in 1927 is causally relevant to my saying 'The hundredth man born in Russia in 1927 is probably still in Russia', which is based on my knowledge of the probabilities. This is why we are happy in the first case to say that I am talking about a specific man, whereas we are doubtful whether it is appropriate to say this in the second case. Again, in cases of misattribution or of conflation examination of causal antecedents can provide us with a reason for saying that someone is talking about one rather than another of several possible candidates. In cases of conflation, two different items figure in a seemingly appropriate way in the causal history of a dossier, which is thus not unambiguously a dossier on either of them.

I do not wish to claim that it is incorrect to say, in those cases where no causal link exists, that the speaker is talking about the item to which the description he uses applies, although I think that as a matter of fact those cases about which we feel intuitive unease are those where there is no clear, unambiguous, causal link to a single item in the world. As I said before, ordinary usage may be permissive on this point. What I claim is that if we wish, for philosophical purposes, to draw a line about some uses of referring phrases, or about some dossiers of descriptions, the presence or absence of a causal link provides a coherent rationale for doing so. In particular I think that in relation to emotions and their objects, such a causal condition is necessary. That is, when we say that an emotion has as its object a particular item in the world because it is elicited by thinking about that item, a causal chain of the kind suggested must be traceable between the item and the associated dossier.

4

I have suggested that both perception and thought are linked causally to the world, and that it is partly by virtue of these causal links that they have the objects that they do. Of course in each case much more is involved than the existence of a causal link between an item in the world and perception or thought. For a person to perceive an item, it is not sufficient that the item should figure in a certain way in the causal genesis of his present sensory state. This sensory state must satisfy further conditions. Similarly in the case of thought. These relations are what I earlier called template relations.

I have restricted my discussion to the cases of perception of an item and thought about an item, as I think that other forms of attention to an item can be understood in terms of these. To what extent has the discussion met the objection raised at the beginning of the chapter? The objection was that my account of how emotions have objects was unhelpful, for it explained this feature of emotions by reference to other types of mental states which themselves had objects – perception, thought, and so on. It explained how emotions link up to the world by reference to mental states which link up to the world in just the same way, and thus did not address itself to the general question of what kind of link this was.

I have tried to show what is involved when a person attends to a particular item in the world, and have thus explored in more detail the link between particular emotions and their objects. If the force of the objection was that my original account was too sketchy, then I may have done something to meet it. For the objector may mean that it is unsatisfactory to explain the link between emotion and object by saying that the emotion must be caused by attention to the object, if the link between attention to the object and the object is left unexamined. If this is how his objection is to be taken, my discussion of the relation between perception and object and between thought and object may have helped to satisfy him.

But this may not be the full force of the objection. Perhaps what worries the objector is some question of the form: How can emotions have objects at all? In this case he will be equally worried by the question: How can perception and thought have objects? He is worried by these questions as aspects of the more general question: How is it that the mind can connect to things outside the mind? How can the mind reach out beyond itself to items in the world? If it is this kind of question that worries him, spelling out in more detail the link between emotions and their objects will fail to satisfy him. Reference to particular causal links between items in the world and mental states does not help to remove his perplexity, for what concerns him is partly how it is that physical causes can have mental effects.

It is not clear what kind of answer might be required to the question, how the mind can reach out beyond itself. Perhaps there is more than one question lurking here. There may be an epistemological question, concerning the basis of claims to knowledge of the outside world. But I think that there is also a more fundamental perplexity, concerning the fact that the mind can, as it were, come into contact with the outside world at all. It is a question of how there can be any kind of interaction between the physical and the mental. How can that which is not mental impinge on that which is?

To answer this question would require a general examination of the nature of consciousness, and of the relation between the mind and behaviour. As this problem has engaged philosophers since the subject began, I hope I will be excused if I lift my hat respectfully and pass by. I think that just because the question is of such great generality and centrality, one can justifiably restrict one's discussion to a lower level. One can plot out more particular connections between the mind and the world, while leaving the general question in abeyance.

Nevertheless we must pause for a moment in this vicinity, for some philosophers have claimed that it is intentionality that is the distinguishing mark of the mental. They have claimed, furthermore, that because this is so, certain general theories of the relationship between the mental and the physical can be ruled summarily out of court. They have argued that intentionality is a property that all mental phenomena have and that all physical phenomena lack, and that no theory which, like materialism and behaviourism, reduces the mental to the physical, can possibly be true.

Such philosophers have used the notion of object more generously than I, in such a way that having an object is equated with being intentional. I have argued for a more restricted use of 'object', to apply only to items really existing in the world. In the next chapter I shall consider whether there is a viable notion of intentionality which has more general application, whether it is a property possessed by all mental phenomena, and whether the existence of this property dooms reductionist theories of the mind before they start. I shall argue that the prospect of such a quick and painless victory is an illusion.

XV

Intentionality

I

In Chapter VI I restricted the range of application of 'object' to items in the world. I said that although well-founded emotions could be said to have an object, malfounded emotions, based on a mistaken existential belief, could not. I said that 'propositional' emotions, like fear that something is the case, did not, according to my usage, have objects. But I suggested that there might be some more comprehensive notion of intentionality such that all these emotions are intentional. I suggested also that emotions might share this property with beliefs, desires, and other mental states and dispositions. Philosophers have generally taken these various types of mental states and dispositions to be importantly similar, and have referred to the respect in which they are similar as their intentionality. Although they have explained this notion by use of object-terminology, it may be possible to offer an alternative account.

The term 'intentionality' itself is a philosophical invention, but its introduction seems intuitively acceptable. At a pre-philosophical level, we do feel that beliefs, desires, and many emotions have something in common, which they share with other mental states, acts and dispositions. When pressed to say what it is that they have in common, the natural reaction is to refer to the fact that a belief must be a belief *that* something is the case, a desire must be a desire *to* do something, anger must be anger *with* someone, and so on. However, at a philosophical level this sort of informal explanation is not sufficient. We must attempt to say in more systematic terms what these various states and dispositions have in common. In view of the objections advanced in Chapter VII, we must resist the temptation to explain the intentionality of beliefs, desires and emotions in terms of the *language* we use to describe them, or to say that what they have in common is that the statements used to report them share a certain logical feature. It is the beliefs, desires and emotions which are intentional, and our account of this notion must have reference to features of these states and dispositions themselves.

2

Apart from 'object', the term most commonly used to explain intentionality is 'content'. Brentano talks, in the passage quoted in Chapter VIII, 1, of 'reference to a content'. To say that beliefs and desires are characterised by *reference* to a content seems misleadingly to suggest that what is involved is a relation of some kind. It would be better, perhaps, to say that beliefs and desires have content, or are contentful. But what is meant by this? What are we saying of beliefs and desires when we say that they have content?

Beliefs and desires are of a dispositional nature. I shall consider first the case of thoughts, which occur at a specific time. When a person has a thought something happens, which we have supposed to be of a symbolic nature, either overt or covert. We would want to say that thoughts are intentional, for if a person has a thought, his thought must have content. But what is the force of saying that a thought has content? What is it about thoughts that makes them intentional?

There are a number of different ways in which particular items can be grouped together or classified. One kind of basis of classification is the possession of similar qualities. Thoughts could be grouped together on the basis of their introspectible or observable qualities, according as what occurs in each case is qualitatively similar or different. Another kind of basis of classification of items is in terms of their relations to other items. Thoughts could be grouped together on a relational basis, for example in terms of their temporal or causal relations to other events. But when a number of thoughts are all thoughts of food, the basis of classification is neither qualitative nor relational. Different people can be thinking of food, even though their thoughts are not at all qualitatively alike. What goes on in each case is not at all the same. So there is a way of classifying thoughts together which is not straightforwardly qualitative or relational, and all thoughts can be grouped together with other thoughts in such a way. I think that this is part of the force of saying that thoughts have content. We say that the particular thoughts that people have are contentful because they can be grouped together with other thoughts in a way which has to do neither with qualitative similarity nor with their possessing similar relations to other items.

Other mental states and dispositions can be classified similarly in a non-qualitative, non-relational way. For dispositions, the account must be modified. With any disposition there will be associated a set of occurrences which are manifestations or actualisations of that disposition. As qualitative classifications of dispositions we must include classifications based on the qualitative similarity of their manifestations. Thus even if two mixtures of gases which are explosive are qualitatively dissimilar, the basis for classifying them together is the qualitative similarity of the manifestations of their explosiveness. But if the beliefs of two people are grouped together as instances of the same belief-type, this is not by virtue of the introspectible or observable similarity of their present states, nor is it by virtue of the qualitative similarity of the behaviour which manifests their beliefs. Nor, yet again, is the basis of classification relational. The desires that people have can also be classified together on a basis which is neither qualitative nor relational. Here we must note a qualification. Desires can be had for specific things. Thus someone can want a specific painting. So if two people are said to have the same desire, the basis for saying this is sometimes relational – they want the same thing, the same painting, for example. Nevertheless in such a case a person's desire can be described non-relationally, without reference to any specific item, and can be grouped together with other desires on a non-relational basis. Other mental states, acts, and dispositions, that we want to call intentional—judgements, suppositions, doubts, conclusions, decisions, intentions, wishes, etc. – share this feature, that they can be classified and compared to states, acts, or dispositions of the same kind on a basis which is neither qualitative nor relational. So also can emotions, even those which, like malfounded and propositional emotions, have no object.

Some human actions fall into classes with a similarly non-qualitative, non-relational basis. Human actions may be grouped together by reference, for example, to the intention with which they are performed. Thus two people can be said to be doing the same thing, like summoning help, or preparing for rain, even though their actions are not qualitatively similar. In this way the philosophical notion of intentionality meets up with the ordinary notion of intention.

Not all mental states fall into classes with a non-qualitative, non-relational basis. Sensations do not, in this sense, have content. If two people are in pain, their pains can be compared and classified in qualitative terms, according to their intensity, or according as they are jabbing, or throbbing, or piercing, or however else they may be. They may also be compared and classified in relational terms, for example in terms of their cause. But there is no further basis for classifying pains which is neither qualitative nor relational. Sensory states, on the other hand, can be classified in the appropriate way. For two people to seem to see the same thing, their sensory states do not have to be qualitatively similar. Nor do their sensory states have to bear the same relation to some other item or items, for they may not be veridical.

3

We use words like 'belief', 'desire' and 'fear' in two ways. We use them to refer to types of mental states and dispositions, and also to particular instances of those types. Thus we may talk of the belief that Labour will win the next election, or the desire to see Rome, or alternatively of Tom's belief that Labour will win the next election, or Dick's desire to see Rome. I have been applying the notions of content and of intentionality to particular mental states and dispositions, the mental states and dispositions of particular people. I have suggested that part of the force of saying that such mental states and dispositions have content, or are intentional, is that they can be classified together with other particular states and dispositions of the same kind on a basis which is neither qualitative nor relational. This suggestion may not seem to be entirely satisfactory. For someone might reasonably ask what it is about thoughts or beliefs or desires that furnishes a basis for classification other than qualitative or relational similarity. How is that all these kinds of mental states and dispositions admit of this sort of classification?

It would be a mistake to assume that there *must* be a single answer to this question. Thoughts, beliefs, desires, sensory states, etc., have in common that they can be classified with other states or dispositions of the same kind on a basis which is not straightforwardly qualitative or relational. It doesn't follow that they must have something further in common, that is, that there must be a generally applicable answer to the question, how such states and dispositions can be classified together in a non-qualitative, non-relational way. It is thinking that there must be some generally applicable answer to this question that leads people to offer pseudo-explanations in terms of intentional objects and the like. Nevertheless, there may be an answer to this question which has general application. To see if there is, we should look individually at the various kinds of mental states and dispositions whose instances fall into classes in the appropriate way.

Thus one can ask of sensory states: how is it that particular sensory states can be classified together other than on the basis of qualitative similarity or common relational properties? For example, how is it that a number of qualitatively dissimilar sensory states can all be states of seeming to see a horse? One can also ask: what is it about this particular sensory state that makes it a state of seeming to see a horse? To answer these questions properly would involve giving an account of perception. Roughly, when someone sees a horse, his visual state must bear a certain relation, let us call it R, to a horse. I have suggested, following Grice, that R is a certain kind of causal relation, that is, that the horse must be involved in a certain way in the causal genesis of the person's visual state. There is a limited range of visual states which could bear relation R to a horse. Someone's visual state is a state of seeming to see a horse if it falls within this range, that is, if it is such that it could under certain specified conditions have had relation R to a horse. What makes qualitatively dissimilar sensory states all states of seeming to see a horse is that they are all states which could bear the relation in question to a horse. They can be qualitatively dissimilar because a horse presents different aspects from different angles and under different conditions. So generally, visual states can be classified together if they are all such that they could have relation R to an item of the same type, the relation being the same whatever type of item is in question. States of seeming to see an item of a type which is nowhere instantiated pose no particular problem. States of seeming to see a unicorn are all such that they could have relation R to a unicorn, if such a beast existed.

In this way sensory states can be classified together even though they are qualitatively dissimilar and bear no common relation to any other item or items. Of course the basis of classification is connected with the qualities that sensory states have and the kinds of ways in which they can be related to other items, but the connection is a highly complex one. Sensory states of the same type are related to one another through their common potential for a certain relation with an item of a certain type.

Now can a relevantly similar account be given of other sorts of mental states and dispositions? Let us take the case of a mental act such as a decision to do something. When someone decides to do A and then does A as a result of his decision, he performs a mental act which bears a certain relation S to his doing A. The relation is, I think, a causal one. What actually occurs when someone decides to do A varies from occasion to occasion, but particular decisions can be classified together as of this type, that is, as decisions to do A, because they could all in certain circumstances bear relation S to an act of doing A. In general, what makes different decisions instances of the same type is that they are all such that they could bear relation S to an action of the same type.

This, of course, is far from being an adequate account of the nature of decisions, or of the relation of decision to action. But I think it can be seen that the accounts outlined for perception and decision are formally similar. In each case there is a relation such that instances of the mental state or act in question can be classified together because they fall within the range of states or acts which could bear that relation to an item of the same type. Now if an account of the same form can be given for all mental states, acts and dispositions which can be classified on a non-qualitative, non-relational basis, to that extent there will be a generally applicable answer to the question, how such states, acts and dispositions can be so classified.

Consider, for example, the case of beliefs, which are dispositional. I think we can say that two people have beliefs of the same type if they are disposed to act in a way which would be appropriate to states of affairs of the same type. If someone believes that it is raining, then he is disposed to act in a way which, if it were raining, would be appropriate to that state of affairs. What kinds of action would be appropriate would, of course, depend on the other circumstances. I do not claim that this is at all satisfactory as an account of belief. As has frequently been pointed out, we can only attribute a belief to someone on the basis of his behaviour if we know something about his other beliefs and his ends of action. But I do not think that this is relevant in the present context. I think that it is sufficient to show that an explanation can be given for the fact that people's beliefs can be classified on a non-qualitative, non-relational basis, which has the requisite formal features. Those who oppose behavioural analyses of belief do not deny that if someone believes that it is raining, then he is disposed to act in a way which, if it were raining, would be appropriate to that state of affairs. What they say is that because to spell out what appropriateness consists in any particular case would involve reference to beliefs, any attempt at analysis of belief along these lines must fail. I do not think that the objection is a valid one, but for present purposes it is not necessary to show this.

I think, though I shall not attempt to prove, that a formally similar account can be given for each kind of mental state, act or disposition to which we wish to attribute intentionality or content. That is, I think that for each kind of mental item there is some relation such that mental items of that kind typically bear that relation to items in the world – things, persons, events, actions, or states of affairs – such that mental items of that kind need not be so related to anything, but such that they are classified into types according to their potential for bearing the relation in question to items of the same type. How it is that qualitatively dissimilar mental items can be related in fact or potentially to an item of the same type will depend on the kind of mental item in question. The explanation may concern, for example, the variety of aspects that a physical object can present to experience, or the many different ways in which an item can be symbolised.

This notion of intentionality has much more general application than the notion of an object outlined in earlier chapters. Every emotion with an object will also be intentional. But in addition malfounded emotions and those which I called propositional will be intentional. As I am using 'content', they can be said to have content. This is to be understood non-relationally, and is quite distinct from the notion of an object. It is not legitimate to say that the object of someone's emotion is part of the content of his emotion. Kenny's distinction between emotions and sensations can be reformulated in terms of intentionality or content, for as I am using the term, all or nearly all emotions are intentional, whereas sensations are not.

4

Brentano claimed that intentionality was the feature which distinguished mental phenomena from physical phenomena. To what extent does this thesis survive on our account? There are two questions: First, are any mental phenomena non-intentional? Secondly, are any physical phenomena intentional? As regards the first, I claimed that sensations such as pain failed to meet the conditions for intentionality. Such sensations pose a problem for Brentano himself. He appears to deal with them by distinguishing between the primary and the secondary object of any mental act, the secondary object being the mental act itself. Even with phenomena such as sensations which have no primary object, there is still a secondary object.[1] However such a manoeuvre is not possible on our account.

The second question is more important, for if at least some mental phenomena are intentional, and no physical phenomena are, this would seem to provide an easy refutation of those doctrines which claim that the mental is just a form of the physical – materialism, behaviourism, etc. Now some physical things seem to meet the conditions I suggested. Words and sentences can be grouped together on a non-qualitative, non-relational basis, namely in terms of their meaning. Similarly pictures can be grouped together according to what they depict. If intentionality is understood in terms of having content, this is not surprising, since one would quite naturally say that words and sentences and pictures have content.

However, even if a criterion of intentionality were produced which applied only to mental states and dispositions, the prospect of such an easy refutation of physicalism would be illusory. It might be the case that there were no *non-mental* phenomena or states which were intentional. But to assume that therefore there are no *physical* phenomena or states which are intentional would be to beg just the point at issue, for if the mental is a form of the physical, then there *are* intentional physical phenomena, namely mental phenomena. For

---

[1] Findlay offers a conflicting, and surely erroneous interpretation: 'Brentano's doctrine, however, goes further in refusing to admit any class of mental state that is *not* thus of something or other: the thrills, pangs, twitches, etc., which are for some paradigms of "experience", would be for him not experiences, not "psychic phenomena", at all.' (J. N. Findlay, *Values and Intentions* (London, 1961), p. 35.)

instance, a behaviourist might claim that a belief is some kind of complicated disposition to behave. If he is right, then there is something which is both physical and intentional, namely this disposition to behave. It is not, of course, something which is both non-mental and intentional, but that is irrelevant. The behaviourist may be wrong, but the fact that beliefs are intentional does not show him to be wrong.

This point holds good whatever account of intentionality is given. It holds good also for Chisholm's attempted linguistic reconstruction of Brentano's thesis. He states the first part of his reconstructed thesis as follows:

Let us say . . . that we do not need to use intentional language when we describe non-psychological, or 'physical', phenomena; we can express all that we know, or believe, about such phenomena in language which is not intentional.[2]

The equation of the non-psychological with the 'physical' seems once again to beg the important questions.

[2] Chisholm, 'Sentences about Believing', p. 129.

XVI

Some interpretative problems

I

I have tried to keep separate issues arising in the philosophy of mind, which concern certain types of mental states and dispositions, from related issues which concern the way we talk about these states and dispositions, and which belong more properly to philosophical logic. Others have not seen these issues as separate, but have discussed the states and dispositions in question in terms of logical properties of the language used to describe them. I argued in Chapter VII that this approach was mistaken, that there are distinct issues involved, and that issues of the first kind must be treated in a substantive way at their own level. Issues of the second kind can then profitably be discussed in the light of what is said about the related area of philosophy of mind. I shall now try to support this claim by examining some problems of interpretation presented by descriptions of mental states and dispositions, and by showing how a solution to these problems connects to the substantive treatment of the phenomena described.

I shall refer to the statements which report mental states and dispositions, and in connection with which interpretative problems arise, as *P*-statements. They can be divided into two classes. The first class, which I shall call *P*1-statements, purport to assign objects to emotions or attitudes. In these the verb is generally followed by a singular term, or by a preposition and singular term. Here are some examples:

> Smith is afraid of his neighbour's dog.
> Smith hates Jones.
> The Smiths are overjoyed at the return of their son.
> I am worried about her continued illness.

The second class – *P*2-statements – includes reports of those emotions which I called propositional, and reports of beliefs, desires, intentions, wishes, etc. The problems to be discussed arise when the clause following the verb contains a referring phrase. Some examples are as follows:

> He was afraid that the burglar was going to attack
> him.
> I am sorry that the Smiths were not there.
> I am afraid to speak to the manager.
> He hopes to see the Queen.
> She is afraid of offending her husband's boss.
> Smith thinks that the King of France is coming to
> the party.
> Smith wants to see the manager.
> Smith wishes that the King of France were here.

2

In the examples given, the main verb is in every case followed by a referring expression – a name or definite description. The question we are concerned with could be put in this form: Do these referring expressions have a genuinely referential function when they occur in such contexts? However, the question as formulated is not entirely clear. There are various aspects of the problem which I shall distinguish, initially in connection with P_1-statements. Consider such a statement, S, which contains a referring expression, r.

(1) Does the truth-value of S depend on r's having a referent or not? That is, does S entail that the result of substituting r for 'X' in 'X exists' is true? If it does not, then surely this is a reason for saying that r does not occur referentially in S. For even where r does have a referent, the truth of S can be established without establishing that this is so. Thus S would not assert a relation between the subject and whatever, if anything, is referred to by r.

To clarify the point at issue, let us reconsider the examples given in Chapter VI, 3. For convenience, I shall restate them here.

(a) Smith, a soft-hearted fellow, is approached by a beggar, who spins him a harrowing tale of his wife's sufferings. Smith believes him, feels intense pity, and gives him money. But suppose that the beggar was deceiving Smith, that he had no wife?

(b) Jones is a timorous man, and when he hears a noise downstairs one night, he thinks it is a burglar. When his wife asks him why he doesn't go down to investigate, he says that he is afraid of the burglar. But suppose that there isn't a burglar?

(c) In *The Magic Flute*, Tamino is shown a picture of Pamina, whereupon he falls in love with her. Consider a variation on the story in which the whole thing is a hoax. The picture is not a portrait of anyone.

I introduced the examples to raise a different question, namely whether in the situations outlined the emotion could be said to have an object. I said that in these situations the emotion cannot be said to have an object, but the further question remains of how the emotion can be reported or described. For instance, in the case of Smith and the beggar, is the statement 'Smith felt sorry for the beggar's wife' true, or does it entail that the beggar had a wife? In the case of Jones and the burglar, when Jones says that he is afraid of the burglar downstairs, is what he says true or false? In *The Magic Flute* variation, can we say that Tamino has fallen in love with the girl in the picture?

(2) The second aspect of the problem concerns substitutivity of identity. Suppose that r does have a referent, and that r^1 is a phrase which refers to the same item. Can we always substitute r^1 for r in S *salva veritate*? Again we can consider some examples.

(d) Suppose that Smith is angry with the man who has stolen his umbrella, and that, unknown to Smith, the man who has stolen his umbrella is the man to whom he is now talking. Does it follow that Smith is angry with the man to whom he is now talking?

(e) Someone is sending Jones anonymous letters threatening to expose him if he does not pay a large sum of money. Jones is afraid of the man who has been sending the letters. Unknown to Jones, the sender of the letters is the man who lives next door. Does it follow that Jones is afraid of the man who lives next door?

(f) Brown has been conducting a long and acrimonious correspondence with his income-tax inspector, so that by now he has come to hate the man. He has also formed the habit of going along to his local pub every Sunday to lunch, where he has struck up an acquaintance with one of the regulars, liking him and thinking him to be a thoroughly good chap. As yet he has discovered neither his name nor his occupation, but in fact this man is none other than his income-tax inspector. Is it true that he hates the man whom he meets every Sunday in the pub, or that he likes his income-tax inspector, or both, or neither?

These two aspects of the problem are related, but not, as is some-times assumed, in this way: that if a statement *S* containing a re-ferring expression *r* entails that *r* has a referent, then substitutivity holds, whereas if *S* does not entail that *r* has a referent, then sub-stitutivity does not hold. This assumption is dubious, for it seems at least theoretically possible that the truth of *S* should depend on *r*'s having a referent, so that in a sense *r* occurs referentially, but that the truth of the statement should also depend on the way in which the referent is referred to, so that substitutivity fails. In this case we might say that the occurrence of *r* is not *purely* referential. The statement 'Smith knows that the mayor of Cambridge is in the next room' may provide an actual case of this. It entails that there is just one mayor of Cambridge, but, one can plausibly claim, the substitution of another description of the mayor of Cambridge might change its truth-value. Possibly also the converse situation could occur.

(3) We can see why the two questions are closely related, for there is a third question similar to the first which is tightly tied to the substitutivity question. The first question was whether *S* entailed that *r* had a referent. The third question is whether *S* entails the existential generalisation of *S* with respect to *r*. The existential generalisation of *S* with respect to *r* is the result of substituting a variable '*x*' for *r* in *S* and preceding the whole by an existential quantifier, '$(\exists x)$'. Thus the existential generalisation of 'He spoke to the mayor' with respect to 'the mayor' is '$(\exists x)$(He spoke to *x*)'. Now it seems that if a statement entails its existential generalisation with respect to a certain referring expression, substitutivity must hold. For instance, if 'Smith knows that the mayor of Cambridge is in the next room' entails '$(\exists x)$(Smith knows that *x* is in the next room)' – to be read 'Something is such that Smith knows that it is in the next room' – the result of substituting any description of the thing in question should be a true statement.[1] Therefore the ques-tion, whether a referring expression must refer, is to be distinguished from the question, whether the existential generalisation of the state-ment with respect to that expression is entailed, or indeed makes sense.

In the examples given, the verb was followed by a name or definite description. Indefinite descriptions can occur in similar con-

[1] Cf. W. V. O. Quine, *From a Logical Point of View* (Cambridge, Mass., 1953), p. 147.

texts. Thus instead of saying 'Smith was afraid of the burglar', we can say 'Smith was afraid of a burglar'. In such cases a comparable problem arises. Since indefinite descriptions are perhaps not strictly speaking referring expressions, the problem is best put in terms of the existential generalisation. That is, if 'Smith is afraid of a burglar' is true, must there exist something of which Smith is afraid?

The same problems arise when a referring expression occurs in the subordinate clause of a $P2$-statement. Thus consider S: 'He was afraid that the burglar was going to attack him.' (1) Does S entail that there was a burglar? (2) Does the conjunction of S with 'The burglar was the local M.P.' entail that he was afraid that the local M.P. was going to attack him? (3) Does S entail '$(\exists x)$(He was afraid that x was going to attack him)'? Referential problems arise also in connection with statements of types other than those mentioned, with statements, for example, employing verbs such as 'look for'.[2]

Since the problems are general ones, concerning any referring expression occurring in a psychological context, the natural presumption is that a unitary account will suffice, i.e. that the same solution will work in every case. I shall suggest that in fact this is not so, that different accounts are suitable for $P1$- and $P2$-statements, and shall try to explain how the difference arises. Initially, however, I shall discuss the problem generally.

3

Let us for the present neglect the possibility of a hybrid, and assume that the choice is between an extensional interpretation of psychological statements whereby a referring expression occurring in a psychological context must have a referent if the statement in which it occurs is to be true, and substitutivity holds, and an intensional interpretation whereby such referring expressions need not have a referent, and substitutivity does not hold. For any psychological statement, the options open to us would then be to say either (i) that the statement admits only of an extensional interpretation, or (ii) that the statement admits only of an intensional interpretation, or (iii) that the statement admits of both interpretations.

[2] Cf. W. V. O. Quine, *Word and Object* (Cambridge, Mass., 1960), Chapter IV, and *From a Logical Point of View*, Chapter VIII.

Most of the discussion of these matters springs from Quine. He himself seems to think that the belief construction at any rate admits of both interpretations.

A construction that may be transparent or opaque is the belief construction, '*a* believes that *p*'. Thus suppose that though

(7) Tom believes that Cicero denounced Catiline,

he is ill-informed enough to think that the Cicero of the orations and the Tully of *De Senectute* were two. Faced with his unequivocal denial of 'Tully denounced Catiline', we are perhaps prepared both to affirm (7) and to deny that Tom believes that Tully denounced Catiline. If so, the position of 'Cicero' in (7) is not purely referential. But the position of 'Cicero' in the part 'Cicero denounced Catiline', considered apart, is purely referential. So 'believes that' (so conceived) is opaque.

At the same time there is an alternative way of construing belief that is referentially transparent. The difference is as follows. In the opaque sense of belief considered above, Tom's earnest 'Tully never denounced Catiline' counts as showing that he does not believe that Tully denounced Catiline, even while he believes that Cicero did. In the transparent sense of belief, on the other hand, Tom's earnest 'Cicero denounced Catiline' counts as showing that he does believe that Tully denounced Catiline, despite his own misguided verbal disclaimer.[3]

Is Quine correct in saying that there are two interpretations of such statements? What support does ordinary usage lend to either interpretation?

(1) On an extensional account, but not on an intensional account, a psychological statement containing a referring expression would imply that that referring expression had a referent. Now if I utter a psychological statement employing a name or definite description I certainly seem to imply that this name or description has a referent. Thus if I say that Smith is angry with the man who stole his bicycle, or that Jones was afraid of the burglar who broke in last night, I seem to imply that someone did steal Smith's bicycle, or that a burglar did break in last night. Someone who heard me would conclude from what I said that this was so, and would surely be justified in doing so. Furthermore, if I found out that I had been mistaken in thinking that there was such a person, I would probably retract or modify my statement.

However, we should not assume that if in saying one thing, I imply something else, it is necessarily the *statement* I make which

[3] Quine, *Word and Object*, p. 145.

carries the implication. Grice has shown that there are several ways in which implications can be carried. For instance, if I say 'My wife is either in the kitchen or in the bedroom', I would normally be taken to imply that I did not know which of the two rooms she was in.[4] But in this case the implication does not result from the conventional force or meaning of what I say. If in fact I did know which of the two rooms she was in, I would not have said something false – rather, I would have said something which although true was misleading. Now similarly it might be the case that although in saying that Smith is angry with the man who stole his bicycle I imply that someone did steal Smith's bicycle, this statement could nonetheless be true even if no-one stole it – the implication would not be carried by the statement, but in some other way. Since we are inquiring into the *meaning* of certain statements, we are concerned only with the implications carried by the statements themselves, and not with those carried in other ways.

Grice gives certain tests to settle how an implication is carried, but unfortunately they do not seem to yield a clear answer in this case. The most relevant test is to see whether or not the implication is cancellable, that is whether or not one can take a form of words for which both what is asserted and what is implied is the same as for 'Smith is angry with the man who stole his bicycle', and then add a further clause withholding commitment from what would otherwise be implied, with the idea of annulling the implication without annulling the assertion.[5] Can one say in this instance, 'Smith is angry with the man who stole his bicycle – of course nobody stole it, the fool has forgotten that he didn't bring it with him'? If this is permissible, even when 'Smith is angry with the man who stole his bicycle' is taken in its normal meaning, then the implication is not a conventional one – it does not result from the meaning of the statement. Unhappily it is not at all clear whether we would say such a thing.

(2) On an extensional account, if a referring expression in a psychological context has a referent, a codesignative term can be substituted for it *salva veritate*. This would not necessarily be so on an intensional account, though some limited substitution might be allowed. The limits of permissible substitution would depend on

[4] 'Causal Theory of Perception', pp. 130–1.
[5] *Ibid.* p. 128.

what particular intensional account was given. Perhaps the governing factor would be the subject's beliefs. A referring expression could occur in a psychological context only if the subject accepted that it had an appropriate reference. Thus 'Smith believes that the mayor of Cambridge is going to be at the reception' would be true only if Smith would assent to the proposition that the mayor of Cambridge was going to be at the reception. It would not be true if, although Smith would assent to the proposition that his future son-in-law was going to be at the reception, he did not know that his future son-in-law was in fact the mayor of Cambridge. Substitution of one term for another codesignative term in a psychological context would only be permitted if the subject believed that they were codesignative.

Now when I make a psychological statement about someone, there does seem to be some kind of implication of acceptance with regard to referring phrases occurring in the statement. Thus if I say that Smith believes that the mayor of Cambridge is going to be at the reception, I do seem to imply that Smith would assent to the contained proposition. It would normally be misleading to say this if Smith would not assent to the contained proposition, but only to the proposition that his future son-in-law was going to be at the reception. Similarly in example (f) in Section 2, concerning Brown and his income-tax inspector, it seems misleading to say that Brown hates the man whom he meets every Sunday in the pub. He shows no sign of hating him when he meets him, chats amiably with him, and so on. But although to say this is misleading, is it false? After all, Brown hates his income-tax inspector, and his income-tax inspector *is* the man whom he meets in the pub, so must he not hate the man whom he meets in the pub?

It is sometimes objected here that adoption of the extensional account would force us to say that Smith both likes and hates the man he meets every Sunday in the pub, and that this is a contradiction so apparent that it needs no argument to show it so. Since no argument is produced to show it so, and since it doesn't seem to me to be a straightforward contradiction, I shall assume that the extensional account cannot be dismissed so easily. Again, some philosophers have taken it to be obvious that the description following a psychological verb such as 'hate' gives what they call 'the description under which' the object is hated, but I shall again assume that the question cannot be settled so easily.

There seems in general to be an implication of acceptance. Nevertheless we do on occasion allow substitution outside the subject's beliefs. Scheffler gives a case suggested to him by Nelson Goodman.

A witness, let us suppose, is asked to identify the culprit (Lightfingered Larry) among seven suspects on the police lineup and, not knowing his proper name, declares truly, 'The third man from the left is the culprit'. Reporting in indirect mode, the attendant states, 'The witness says that Lightfingered Larry is the culprit'... [This] is surely true, even if the witness fails to affirm its that-content under questioning.[6]

Again, if someone bursts into the shop in which I work demanding to see the manager, I can surely truly call out to the office 'There's a man here who wants to see Mr. Robinson', even if the intruder does not know the manager's name.

(3) On an extensional account, but not on an intensional account, a psychological statement entails its existential generalisation with respect to a referring expression contained in it. On an intensional account, the existential generalisation does not even make sense. The linguistic facts relevant here concern uses of expressions such as 'someone'. As Quine points out, we have to be careful here, for there are ambiguities of scope. The existential generalisation of 'Smith believes that the mayor of Cambridge is going to be at the reception' with respect to 'the mayor of Cambridge', if there be any such, is not 'Smith believes that someone is going to be at the reception', but 'Someone is such that Smith believes that he is going to be at the reception'.[7]

Undoubtedly we sometimes do use 'someone' as the extensional account would suggest. As Quine says, 'See what urgent information the sentence "There is someone whom I believe to be a spy" imparts, in contrast to "I believe that someone is a spy" (in the weaker sense of "I believe there are spies")'.[8]

Again, we sometimes make statements like 'There's someone here who I'd like you to meet,' or 'She's in love with someone, though I'm not sure who'.

(4) A related point concerns pronominal cross-reference. We sometimes use personal pronouns after a psychological verb to refer

---

[6] I. Scheffler, 'On Synonymy and Indirect Discourse', *Philosophy of Science*, XXII (1955), p. 42. The example is in terms of 'says', but it will surely work for 'thinks' as well.

[7] Cf. Quine, *Word and Object*, p. 147.   [8] *Ibid*. p. 148.

back to a description occurring in a previous clause or sentence. Thus we might say 'Mary dashed away because she saw the boss coming. She is terrified of him', or 'Jones thinks that a burglar broke in last night and is afraid that he will come back to-night'. This usage points to an extensional interpretation.

(5) Referring phrases in psychological contexts are sometimes used to characterise the person referred to. The statements in which they occur are intended to be *about* the referent of the name or description. Thus if asked to describe the boss, I might say that he is big and tough-looking, and that all his subordinates are afraid of him. Or I might say of a politician that everyone thinks that he will become Prime Minister some day. This again seems to suggest an extensional interpretation.

4

The considerations adduced in the previous section seemed sometimes to support an extensional interpretation of P-statements, sometimes to support an intensional interpretation, and sometimes to lend no firm support to either. Why can we not just rest the matter here, and say that P-statements can sometimes be understood extensionally, and sometimes intensionally? For several reasons more ought to be said. Even if P-statements could be understood in different ways on different occasions, certain questions would remain to be answered.

(1) If these statements can be understood in different ways on different occasions, does it follow that they are ambiguous, that is, that their meaning differs on these different occasions? The fact that different interpretations can be put upon a statement can sometimes be accounted for without postulating a plurality of meanings or senses. Might this not be such a case?

(2) If P-statements are genuinely ambiguous, this might be explained in several ways. We might have to say that the psychological verbs themselves – 'believe', 'want', 'fear', etc. – are ambiguous. Alternatively we might be able to account for the sentence-ambiguity without needing to postulate word-ambiguity.

(3) If P-statements admit of different interpretations, how do these relate to one another? Is there a systematic relation which holds in every case?

(4) If *P*-statements admit of different interpretations, we must try to explain this fact in terms of features of the states and dispositions which the statements report, i.e. by reference to the related area of the philosophy of mind. How parochial this fact about *P*-statements is may depend on whether such an explanation is forthcoming. Is it just a fact about certain statements in English, or can we expect that statements which serve the same function in other languages are likely to be relevantly similar?

(5) If *P*-statements admit of more than one interpretation, why are we not normally in doubt as to how they are to be taken? Why do we nearly always take them extensionally in one set of circumstances, and intensionally in another set of circumstances? Why, for example, if someone utters a *P*-statement containing a name or definite description, does he normally seem to imply that something exists answering to that name or description?

5

I shall take the first question first, and ask whether all the linguistic facts can be accounted for on the supposition that *P*-statements are not ambiguous. In this case any *P*-statement would have only one standard conventional meaning. If we said that, standardly understood, *P*-statements were extensional, we would have to explain why they sometimes seem to be intensional. We would have to explain why we sometimes make and accept *P*-statements containing referring expressions which lack a referent – for surely we sometimes do – why we are reluctant to allow complete substitutivity, and why there is commonly an acceptance implication.

Theoretically we could try taking either the intensional or the extensional account as basic. For several reasons I shall adopt the latter course. First, the considerations adduced in Section 3 were more favourable to a basically extensional account. Some seemed incompatible with a wholly intensional one. Secondly, our discussion of the related issues in the philosophy of mind suggests an extensional account, at any rate for *P*1-statements. I shall return to this point later. Thirdly, it seems to me as a matter of principle preferable to give a basically extensional account if possible. Fourthly, as will be seen in the next chapter, there is another class of psychological statements whose members seem at first to admit of two interpretations, but can be plausibly said to have only one standard meaning, and that an extensional one. This class is sufficiently similar to the class under consideration to suggest that the solution might be transferable.

XVII

The extensional approach

I

The class of statements mentioned at the end of the last chapter is the class of perception statements. The linguistic facts again provide *prima facie* grounds for saying that such statements admit both of an extensional and of an intensional interpretation. However, these linguistic facts can be reconciled with the claim that taken in their standard meaning perception statements are extensional. We can explain, consistently with this claim, how it is sometimes legitimate to understand these statements intensionally.

It is a contentious question whether a statement of the form 'Smith sees an *F*' entails that there exists an *F* which Smith sees. Without doubt many examples can be given of situations where the utterance of such a statement seems to lack this implication. For instance, talking of a drunk man, or of a man suffering an hallucination, one might say 'He sees pink rats', and not imply that there are pink rats which he sees. Again, one talks of seeing spots in front of one's eyes when there are no spots in front of one's eyes. Further examples are given by Miss Anscombe in her article 'The Intentionality of Sensation'.[1]

Confronted with such linguistic phenomena, some philosophers have argued that in the primary sense of 'see', 'Smith sees an *F*' does not carry an implication of existence,[2] while others have claimed that there are two senses of 'see', in one of which statements of this kind carry an implication of existence, and in the other of which they do not. But these phenomena can be reconciled with

---

[1] In R. J. Butler (ed.), *Analytical Philosophy II* (Oxford, 1965). By 'sensation' she means perception. She calls intentionality a grammatical feature, though I do not think she has in mind quite what I mean by 'intensionality'.

[2] When Miss Anscombe says that verbs of sense perception 'are intentional or essentially have an intentional aspect' ('The Intentionality of Sensation', p. 169), she seems to be adopting this position.

the claim that there is only one sense of 'see', and that taken in its standard meaning a statement of the form 'Smith sees an F' carries an implication of existence. To account for apparent counter-examples, appeal is made to the notion of ellipsis.[3] In the aberrant cases, we say, 'He sees pink rats' is being used elliptically for 'He seems to see pink rats', or 'It is with him as if he saw pink rats', 'I see spots in front of my eyes' is being used elliptically for 'I seem to see spots in front of my eyes', and so on.

The claim that particular utterances of a sentence are elliptical will be tenable only if certain conditions are fulfilled. First, of course, the ellipsis must be less cumbersome than the original. But secondly, the ellipsis must be made only where there is no danger of confusion, that is, where there is no risk that the sentence might be understood non-elliptically. In the aberrant uses of perception sentences, I believe that these conditions are satisfied. Consider the kind of situation in which someone might use a perception sentence, and not seem to imply that the referring phrase following the perception verb has a referent. One such situation is where the speaker is reporting a dream. Here there is no risk of confusion, since he will have prefaced his narration with some locution such as 'Last night I dreamed that . . .' In other cases the speaker knows that the hearer knows certain relevant facts about the person referred to – that he is drunk, or that he has just taken mescaline, or that he is liable to suffer delusions, or that he is in a typical illusory situation – and the conversational interest is not in what he actually sees, but in what he seems to see.[4] If the speaker knows that the hearer knows the fact in question – and perhaps also that the hearer knows that the speaker knows this – he knows that there is no risk that his utterance will be taken non-elliptically. Again, there are cases where what is said to be seen is such that the speaker knows that the hearer knows that the speaker believes that no such things exist. Thus I might say 'Smith saw the ghost again last night', or 'Jones saw a unicorn in the garden this morning', speaking elliptically, if I know that my audience knows that I do not believe there are any ghosts or unicorns, and thus that I cannot be intending the sentence in question in its standard meaning.

[3] I think that the idea of appealing to ellipsis to explain such perception statements was first suggested to me by J. F. Bennett.

[4] This will deal with Miss Anscombe's cases, like the one where the oculist says 'Move these handles until you see the bird in the nest'.

It appears that the existence-implication is only absent when the context, linguistic or otherwise, makes clear that the sentence is being used elliptically. If the use of a perception sentence could be taken non-elliptically, it is so taken. If I say 'Jones saw a lion in the garden this morning', and if there is nothing about Jones or about the situation known to the hearer which would suggest that Jones was suffering a delusion, the hearer will justifiably take me to be saying that there was a lion in the garden which was seen by Jones.

The linguistic facts can, therefore, be explained on the assumption that perception sentences have only one standard meaning, but can sometimes be used elliptically. If anything more is needed to show that this is a *correct* explanation, it is perhaps this: that ellipsis is a commonly occurring phenomenon, and that the nature and function of language are such that it is a natural phenomenon. The object of language is communication, and if certain facts can be communicated more simply and shortly by contraction, and there is no danger of confusion, then it is natural that such contraction should occur.

2

Appeal to ellipsis thus enables us to reconcile with the linguistic facts the claim that perception sentences standardly understood are extensional. These sentences are sufficiently similar to P-sentences to give some grounds for hope that the latter can be dealt with in the same way. This can be seen if we examine the cases in slightly more detail.

To take the case of seeing, a statement of the form 'Smith is seeing an F', standardly understood, will be true only if both subjective conditions – conditions concerning the subject alone – and objective conditions – conditions concerning things other than the subject, or the relation between him and things other than him – are satisfied. The subjective conditions will concern Smith's visual state. The objective conditions will be that an F should exist, and that it should play a certain kind of causal role in the genesis of Smith's visual state. When 'Smith is seeing an F' is used standardly, both the subjective and the objective conditions will be satisfied. When it is used elliptically for 'Smith seems to see an F', or 'It is with Smith as if he were seeing an F', the subjective conditions alone need be satisfied.

Similarly a P-statement of the form, let us say, 'Smith is angry with the F', understood extensionally, will be true only if both subjective and objective conditions are satisfied. Smith must be in a particular present state, and there must exist something which is the F and is related in a certain kind of way to his present state. Since this parallel exists with the perception case, it seems plausible to say that 'Smith is angry with the F', standardly understood, is extensional, and that when understood intensionally, it is an ellipsis for something of the form 'Smith seems to be angry with the F', or 'It is with Smith as if he were angry with the F', where this means that the subjective conditions for Smith's being angry with the F are satisfied. It might be objected that whereas statements of the form 'Smith seems to see an F' are sometimes made, we never use 'Smith seems to be angry with the F' in this way – we might use it to cast doubt on the anger, not on the object – and that the claim that certain uses of a sentence are elliptical will be plausible only if the fully spelt-out version is something that we might actually say. However, I do not think that this is a valid objection. If the fully spelt-out version seems involved, this could itself explain why we use the ellipsis. Besides, it is just not clear how we do describe malfounded emotions.

What has been said so far suggests that the claim that 'Smith is angry with the F' standardly entails that the F exists can be reconciled with our occasional acceptance of such a statement when this condition is not satisfied. It may also help to explain the apparent reluctance to allow complete substitutivity of identity, but about this more can be said, for such reluctance can be partly explained by appeal to Grice's notion of conversational point. There may be a general presumption that if someone has a choice of descriptions by means of which to refer to a particular person or thing, and if one of these descriptions is for some reason conversationally more appropriate than the others, he will choose that one. Conversely, if one description is the natural or normal one to use, then if someone chooses another less natural or normal description, he implies that there is some conversational point to his doing so. For instance, the normal way of referring to Harold Wilson is as 'Harold Wilson' or 'the Leader of the Opposition'. If one chooses another description, such as 'the M.P. for Huyton', or 'the President of the Board of

Trade under Attlee', one seems to imply that it is conversationally relevant that Harold Wilson is M.P. for Huyton, or was President of the Board of Trade under Attlee, i.e. that one's audience is concerned with him or interested in him in this capacity rather than in any other.

Similarly in the cases we are considering, the natural description to use in reporting Smith's emotions may be a description which he knows to apply to the object. In Chapter xi, 1, we saw that when a person feels an emotion, his subjective state in a sense determines what kind of object his emotion could have. To speak metaphorically, there is a hole which only a certain kind of object could fill. Given that an object does fill the hole, it will satisfy many descriptions such that his subjective state does not demand an object answering to *those* descriptions. The natural way to refer to the object of an emotion would be by means of the descriptions by virtue of which it fills the hole. One would only choose some other description if there were a point to one's doing so – if, for instance, only by doing so would one enable one's audience to identify the object of the emotion.

In addition, of course, the purpose of describing Smith's emotions may be to give a guide to the sort of thing he is likely to do or say, in which case the choice of referring phrase will be important. We are interested in knowing what emotion Smith feels towards Jones, whether, for example, he is afraid of him or angry with him, partly because it enables us to predict how Smith may behave towards Jones, what kinds of thing he may say about him, and so on. To refer to the object of an emotion by a particular description implies that if the person who felt the emotion encountered the object under that description – if, say, he were told that the so-and-so was coming – he would display the appropriate behaviour towards him. If the description chosen is such that the person does not know that the object satisfies it, this condition is not fulfilled. To return to the examples given in Chapter xvi, 2, we could explain in this way why in (e) it is misleading to say that Jones is afraid of the man next door, and how in (f) it could be true that Brown hates the man whom he meets every Sunday in the pub, and that he likes his income-tax inspector, yet could still be misleading to say either of these things without qualification.

Again, looking at Scheffler's example, cited in Chapter xvi, 3, (2), where a *P*-statement is uttered and the acceptance-implication is lacking, one finds, as is to be expected on this account, that the interest is in the object rather than in the subject. The interest is in Lightfingered Larry, and in whether or not the witness identifies him as the culprit – how the witness would refer to him is irrelevant. Similarly the point of shouting out 'There's a man here who wants to see Mr Robinson' is to summon Mr Robinson, and it doesn't matter that the man looking for him doesn't know that he is called Robinson.

3

From the considerations adduced in the previous section we might conclude that a basically extensional account is as plausible for *P*-statements as for perception statements. It is true that many philosophers have considered it *obvious* that such statements are intensional, but that in itself does not prove anything. However the discussion in this chapter has been chiefly in terms of *P*1-statements. There are reasons for thinking that even if *P*2-statements admit of a standard extensional interpretation, they must also admit of a standard intensional interpretation.

(1) Quine attempts to prove that the belief context must sometimes be referentially opaque, i.e. that belief statements must sometimes admit of an intensional interpretation.[5] He claims that if the belief context were always referentially transparent, then one could show that if someone believes anything, he believes everything, which is absurd. His proof utilises a general difficulty that any extensional account would face in regard to identity statements. On an extensional account, 'Smith believes that the author of *Waverley* is the author of *Waverley*', together with 'The author of *Waverley* is the author of *Ivanhoe*', would entail 'Smith believes that the author of *Waverley* is the author of *Ivanhoe*', a result which is surely unacceptable.

Unfortunately there are defects in Quine's discussion which render the force of his proof slightly dubious. His explanation of referential transparency is as follows:

Referential transparency has to do with constructions; modes of containment, more specifically, of singular terms or sentences in singular

[5] Quine, *Word and Object*, pp. 148–9.

terms or sentences. I call a mode of containment Φ referentially transparent if, whenever an occurrence of a singular term t is purely referential in a term or sentence ψ(t), it is purely referential also in the containing term or sentence Φ (ψ(t)).[6]

The fact that the descriptions 'the F' and 'the G' do not occur in a purely referential way in the sentence 'Tom believes that the F is the G' would only show the belief construction here to be referentially opaque if these descriptions occur in a purely referential way in the contained sentence 'The F is the G'. But do they? Quine seems to think that the occurrence of a term is purely referential if it is 'used as a means simply of specifying its object, or purporting to, for the rest of the sentence to say something about'.[7] Taking this at its face value might lead one to question whether in identity statements descriptions occur purely referentially. If I say that the author of *Waverley* is the author of *Ivanhoe*, the description 'the author of *Waverley*' does not seem to be used *simply* as a means of specifying its object. Something seems to depend on which particular means of specifying the object is chosen. To put it another way, one might be inclined to say that 'The author of *Waverley* is the author of *Ivanhoe*' is not really a statement about the author of *Waverley*, but is in some sense about the descriptions.

However the *criterion* of pure referentiality which Quine gives is that substitutivity of identity should hold. This certainly holds for descriptions occurring in identity statements. From 'The author of *Waverley* is the author of *Ivanhoe*', together with 'The author of *Waverley* is Scott', it follows that Scott is the author of *Ivanhoe*. If the criterion is adequate, then the belief context must on occasion be referentially opaque. But what we have said may cast doubt on the adequacy of this criterion.

(2) Whether or not Quine's argument is valid as it stands is not of crucial importance, for other considerations suggest that $P2$-statements must admit of an intensional interpretation. An extensional account seems to work as well for perception statements whether the verb is followed by an indefinite description or by a name or definite description. Indeed the examples we considered were all of the former kind. $P1$-statements are similar in this respect. 'Smith is angry with a man who stole his bicycle' seems to imply its existential generalisation with respect to 'a man who stole his

[6] *Ibid*. p. 144.   [7] *Ibid*. pp. 142–3.

bicycle' in just those circumstances where 'Smith is angry with the man who stole his bicycle' implies the equivalent existential generalisation. *P2*-statements, however, are different. Consider the statement 'Tom wants to ride a horse'. This might be taken to mean that there is some particular horse which Tom wants to ride, but it would more commonly be taken to mean just that Tom wants his present state of not riding a horse to cease, without much caring how. Whereas if someone said 'Smith is angry with a man', and were asked 'Which man?', he would reply by referring to a particular man, if someone said 'Tom wants to ride a horse', and were asked 'Which horse?', he would more often than not reply 'Any horse', or 'No horse in particular'. Furthermore it requires no special context for 'Tom wants to ride a horse' to be taken in the second way. The case is rather the reverse. In any normal situation someone who said 'Tom wants to ride a horse', or 'Tom wants to eat a steak', would not be taken to mean that Tom has some particular horse or steak in mind. This seems characteristic of *P2*-statements containing indefinite descriptions. If I say, for instance, that Smith thinks that a man has jumped more than 25 feet, I might be taken as implying that there is some particular man whom Smith thinks to have jumped more than 25 feet, but more probably I would not be so taken.

Thus whereas a perception statement or a *P1*-statement containing an indefinite description would normally be taken to imply the relevant existential generalisation, a similar *P2*-statement would not. This gives reason to believe that *P2*-statements must admit of a standard intensional interpretation. One suggestion is unacceptable, namely that the standard interpretation of *P2*-statements containing names and definite descriptions is extensional, while that of *P2*-statements containing indefinite descriptions is intensional. Apart from its intrinsic implausibility, this will not do, for insofar as one can interpret the former statements extensionally, one must also be able to interpret the latter statements extensionally. In general, if x has relation R to y, and y is an F, it follows that x has relation R to an F. For instance, if x is next to y, and y is a man, then x is next to a man. Therefore if Tom wants to ride Dobbin, where this is taken extensionally, and Dobbin is a horse, it follows that Tom wants to ride a horse, where this is also taken extensionally.

(3) The Russellian expansion of a statement of the form 'The F is G' is '$(\exists x)(Fx \,\&\, (y)(Fy \supset y=x) \,\&\, Gx)$'. If we look at the

Russellian expansions of P-statements, we notice another asymmetry between P_1-statements and at least some P_2-statements. Consider the P_1-statement:

A is angry with the F.

The only natural Russellian expansion seems to be

$(\exists x)(Fx \ \& \ (y)(Fy \supset y = x) \ \& \ A$ is angry with $x)$.

But when we take a P_2-statement like

A believes that the F is G,

there seem to be two possible Russellian expansions:

(i) $(\exists x)(Fx \ \& \ (y)(Fy \supset y = x) \ \& \ A$ believes that x is $G)$.
(ii) A believes that $(\exists x)(Fx \ \& \ (y)(Fy \supset y = x) \ \& \ Gx)$.

This also suggests that even if P_1-statements admit of only one interpretation, P_2-statements admit of two. Either (i) or (ii) could be naturally contracted into 'A believes that the F is G'.

These considerations taken together suggest that although we can give a basically extensional account of P_1-statements, as of perception statements, we must allow that P_2-statements admit of more than one standard interpretation. I shall later try to explain the difference between these two classes of P-statements.

4

If P_2-statements admit of more than one conventional interpretation, then they are ambiguous, and we must account for this ambiguity. Sentence-ambiguity may arise in various ways. It may result from the ambiguity of some word in the sentence. If any words are ambiguous here, it would be the psychological verbs, 'believe', 'want', etc. In the passage quoted in Chapter xvi, 3, Quine talked of different *senses* of belief, and thus seemed to attribute the sentence-ambiguity to word-ambiguity. But there are other possible explanations for sentence-ambiguity. It may result from ambiguity of syntax rather than from ambiguity of sense. The ambiguities we are concerned with are *systematic* in a way which suggests that they are probably syntactical. It is not just sentences involving a particular word that are ambiguous, but a class of similar sentences involving a number of different words – 'believe', 'think', 'desire', 'hope', etc. To attribute the ambiguity of all P_2-statements to a common ambiguity of syntax would be a much simpler explanation than to postulate a large number of word-ambiguities.

The task of displaying and accounting for syntactical ambiguities belongs largely, I think, to linguists and grammarians rather than philosophers. But it might seem somewhat evasive and unsatisfactory to transfer the responsibility at this point, to assume that linguists will be able to account for the ambiguities under consideration as syntactical. So I shall outline a possible account that might be given for one class of $P2$-statements, those involving 'think'. Even if the particular account that I shall outline is not itself adequate, it will suffice to show that an explanation in terms of syntactical ambiguity is very probably available. I shall try to render the ambiguity of these statements comprehensible by referring to the treatment that would be accorded at a substantive level to the states of affairs they report. I shall also return to the questions raised in Chapter xvi, 4.

XVIII

Syntactical ambiguity

I

I shall apply to the present case some ideas which H. P. Grice developed in a course on Reference.[1] One of his objects in this course was to assess the extent to which formulae of classical logic, or some slight extension of this, can provide one with an elucidation of the conventional force of certain expressions in ordinary speech. Since it was a general methodological principle of his that senses are not to be multiplied beyond necessity, he wished to keep to a minimum the number of conventional forces a sentence could have, and to explain such ambiguity as there was in terms of ambiguity of syntax rather than of sense. At the end of the course he outlined a way of dealing with syntactical ambiguities which may be relevant here. He thought that one might arrive at a solution to some of the problems that concerned him by drawing a distinction between the symbolism of *Principia Mathematica*, and, constructed side by side with it, a closely analogous form of artificial English, which he referred to as 'basic English'. Suppose, for instance, that one wants to know how to interpret a sentence like 'Pegasus does not fly'. (As Pegasus does not exist, is this sentence true or false?) One could say:

(1) If some completion of an open sentence S of basic English can be assigned a truth-value, then the completion of S by 'Pegasus' can also be assigned a truth-value.

(2) 'Flies(Pegasus)' is a completion of the open sentence in basic English 'Flies (x)'.

[1] I attended this course in Oxford in the Michaelmas Term of 1966. It should be clearly understood that what I represent Grice as saying is no more than my present impression of what he said, and is not to be taken as an accurate account of his views at the time. Still less is it to be taken as an indication of what he now thinks on these matters. Should there be any worth in these ideas, however, the credit is of course Grice's.

(3) The completed sentence in basic English 'Not (flies (Pegasus))' can be generated in more than one way.

(a) One can generate it by first completing 'Flies(x)' by substituting 'Pegasus' for 'x', and then prefixing 'not'.

(b) One can generate it by prefixing 'not' to 'Flies(x)', and then completing the resulting open sentence by substituting 'Pegasus' for 'x'.

Thus whereas in (a) the open sentence 'Flies(x)' is predicated on 'Pegasus', and the resulting completed sentence is then negated, in (b) the open sentence 'Not(flies(x))' is predicated on 'Pegasus'. Truth-values only start being assigned when a completed sentence is reached. If an open sentence is completed by being predicated on a singular term which lacks a referent, the resulting completed sentence is false. So in (b), 'Not(flies(Pegasus))' is false, whereas in (a), it is the result of negating the false sentence 'Flies(Pegasus)', and is therefore true. In assigning a truth-value to a sentence such as 'Not(flies(Pegasus))', one must take into consideration the route whereby it has been generated.

The point is that basic English has different formation rules to the *Principia* system. A sentence in basic English is generated by starting with a simple open sentence, and performing certain operations on it. The formation rules are such that the same final sentence can sometimes be reached from two different starting-points. That is, one can take two different simple open sentences – or even the same simple open sentence – and perform two different sets of operations on them, and arrive at the same result. If one takes the equivalent logical formulae, and performs the equivalent sets of operations on them, the two paths will lead to different results. In this way the final sentence in basic English will correspond to more than one formula in the logical system. This shows how a sentence in basic English can be ambiguous, i.e. can admit of more than one interpretation in the logical system, even though no word-ambiguity is involved. It seems fair to call this an ambiguity of syntax.

Ordinary English differs from basic English in that it lacks explicit formation rules. Basic English can most usefully be seen as a way of rewriting ordinary English so as better to display its logical structure, while still retaining the ambiguities of ordinary English. This representation of ordinary English by basic English is justified to the extent that it illuminates the difficulties we have in settling on a unique interpretation of ordinary English sentences. For instance, 'Not(flies(Pegasus))' is supposed to be a representation in basic English of the ordinary English sentence 'Pegasus does not fly'. We are in fact uncertain what truth-value to assign to this sentence. We might view it as denying that Pegasus flies, when it would be true; on the other hand, we might view it in a different way, as purporting to say of Pegasus that he is a non-flyer, when it would be false. It helps to explain our uncertainty if we see this sentence in the light of the basic English equivalent, which can be generated in two ways, and whose truth-value depends on how it is generated.

2

Grice had time in his course only to apply this idea to negated sentences. Before seeing what light it sheds on sentences containing psychological verbs, I would like to expand and explore a little.

In basic English, there are two types of formation move.

(1) One can predicate an open sentence on a name or description. For instance, one can predicate 'Flies(x)' or 'Not(flies(x))' on 'Pegasus' or 'the bird in my hand'.

(2) If one has an open or completed sentence, one can form a new open or completed sentence by applying a certain operator to the original. For instance, one can prefix 'not' to 'Flies(x)' or to 'Flies (Pegasus)'.

In the logical system there will be equivalent moves. For example, the move equivalent to predication of an open sentence on a definite description will be Russellian. That is, we say that moving from '$G(x)$' to 'G(the F)' in basic English is equivalent to moving from 'Gx' to '$(\exists x)(Fx \ \& \ (y)(Fy \supset y = x) \ \& \ Gx)$' in the logical system. In this way we can combine a basically Russellian account of definite descriptions with the recognition that some sentences employing definite descriptions allow of more than one interpretation. Take the sentence 'The F does not fly', which seems to admit of two interpretations, such that if there is nothing which is the F, it is true on one interpretation and false on the other. The basic English equivalent is 'Not(flies(the F))' This can be generated in two ways.

1 Flies(x).
   Flies(the F) $= (\exists x)(Fx \ \& \ (y)(Fy \supset y = x) \ \& \ \text{flies}(x))$.
   Not(flies(the$F$)) $= \sim (\exists x)(Fx \ \& \ (y)(Fy \supset y = x) \ \& \ \text{flies}(x))$.

2   Flies(x).
    Not(flies(x)).
    Not(flies(the F)) = ($\exists x$)(Fx & (y)($Fy \supset y = x$) & $\sim$ flies(x)).

We can say that any predication of an open sentence on a singular term in basic English is equivalent to an existential quantification in the parallel logical system. Thus we can say that moving from '$G(x)$' to 'G(an F)' is equivalent to moving from 'Gx' to '($\exists x$)(Fx & Gx)', and that moving from '$G(x)$' to '$G(a)$' is equivalent to moving from 'Gx' to '($\exists x$)($x = a$ & Gx)'.

This theory allows us to explain how a sentence can admit of different interpretations even though no word in it is ambiguous. The interpretation we place on 'Not(flies(the F))' will depend on the route by which we take it to have been generated. This is essentially another way of saying that how we interpret this sentence depends on what we take to be the predicate in the sentence. Clearly basic English sentences can be of any degree of complexity. A completed sentence 'G(the F)' of the first degree of complexity will only admit of one interpretation. A completed sentence '$O(G$(the F))' of the second degree of complexity will admit of two possible interpretations, a completed sentence '$O*(O(G$(the F)))' of the third degree of complexity will admit of three possible interpretations, and so on. The theory is really a way of mapping English sentences which are systematically ambiguous onto a logical system which permits no ambiguity, a way which illuminates and shows to be systematic the ambiguity of the English sentences.

The justification for taking basic English to be a valid representation of ordinary English is the philosophical illumination to be derived from viewing ordinary English sentences as having this kind of structure. Viewing negated English sentences like this does appear to be illuminating and helpful. But by itself this would not be sufficient to justify the whole enterprise, to show it to be more than an ad hoc concoction that happened to work in this case. It derives its validity from the fact that it can be extended into other areas. Before turning to sentences involving 'think', I shall test it against some other non-psychological cases.

Consider first conditional sentences involving referring expressions. Does a statement of the form 'If the F is G, then p', or of the form 'If p, then the F is G', entail that there is just one F? In other words, if there is nothing which is the F, must such a statement be false? Once again we seem to have inclinations either way. This can be explained by the theory, for 'If p, then $(G(\text{the } F))$' can be generated in two ways.

1 $G(x)$
   $G(\text{the } F) = (\exists x)(Fx \ \& \ (y)(Fy \supset y = x) \ \& \ Gx).$
   If p, then $(G(\text{the } F)) = $ if p then $(\exists x)(Fx \ \& \ (y)(Fy \supset y = x)$ $\& \ Gx).$
2 $G(x)$
   If p, then $(G(x))$
   If p, then $(G(\text{the } F)) = (\exists x)(Fx \ \& \ (y)(Fy \supset y = x) \ \& \ $ if p then $Gx).$

A statement of the form 'If the F is G, then the H is J' can be generated by starting either with '$G(x)$' or with '$J(x)$', and three interpretations can be derived.

The second example involves introducing a new but intuitively acceptable move or formation procedure. If the theory is any good, it should work not only for singular terms, but also for class terms occurring in the same context. A statement like 'All dogs are not edible' seems to admit of two interpretations, for it can either mean that there are some dogs which are not edible, or that there are no dogs which are edible. Can these two interpretations be derived in the theory?

They can, if we say that the move from '$G(x)$' to '$G(\text{all } Fs)$' in basic English is equivalent to the move from 'Gx' to '$(x)(Fx \supset Gx)$' in the logical system. We then have:

1 Edible(x)
   Edible(all dogs) $= (x)(x$ is a dog $\supset x$ is edible).
   Not(edible(all dogs)) $= \sim (x)(x$ is a dog $\supset x$ is edible).
2 Edible(x)
   Not(edible(x))
   Not(edible(all dogs)) $= (x)(x$ is a dog $\supset \sim (x$ is edible)).

These are the two desired interpretations.

3

I argued in the last chapter that certain statements containing psychological verbs are systematically ambiguous. They can be interpreted either extensionally or intensionally. I shall consider one particular class of such statements, those of the form '*A* thinks that *p*', and shall apply the theory to them. The idea is that '*A* thinks that' is an operator like 'not', which can be applied to open or completed sentences to form new open or completed sentences. '*A* thinks that the *F* is *G*' will be equivalent to the basic English sentence '*A* thinks that (*G*(the *F*))', and will admit of two possible interpretations:

1   $G(x)$
$G(\text{the F}) = (\exists x)(Fx \ \& \ (y)(Fy \supset y = x) \ \& \ Gx).$
A thinks that $(G(\text{the F})) = A$ thinks that $(\exists x)(Fx \ \& \ (y)(Fy \supset y = x) \ \& \ Gx).$
2   $G(x)$
A thinks that $(G(x))$
A thinks that $(G(\text{the F})) = (\exists x)(Fx \ \& \ (y)(Fy \supset y = x) \ \& \ A$ thinks that $(G(x))).$

On the first interpretation, the sentence would mean that *A* thinks that there is something which is the *F* and is *G*. Taken in this intensional way, it would not entail that there exists something which is the *F*, and substitution would only be permitted within the limits of *A*'s beliefs. On the second interpretation, the sentence would mean that there is something which is the *F* and which *A* thinks to be *G*. Complete substitutivity of identity would hold, i.e. any description of the F could be substituted *salva veritate*. Thus the theory shows how the sentence can admit of both an extensional and an intensional interpretation, and how the ambiguity can properly be called syntactical.

The sentence '*A* thinks that all dogs are edible' also seems to admit of two interpretations. It can mean either that *A* thinks that it is true that all dogs are edible, or that it is true of all dogs that *A* thinks that they are edible (whether or not he recognises them as dogs and whether or not he thinks mistakenly that there may be dogs which he has not encountered and which are not edible). The theory can account for this too, for it yields the following two interpretations:

1   *A* thinks that $(x) (x$ is a dog $\supset x$ is edible).
2   $(x) (x$ is a dog $\supset A$ thinks that x is edible).

To show conclusively that the ambiguity of '*A* thinks that

the *F* is *G*' is syntactical, and that there is no need to say that 'thinks' is ambiguous, a further step is necessary. We must show that the operator '*A* thinks that' which operates on predicates is the same as the operator '*A* thinks that' which operates on completed sentences. How can this be shown?

A comparable question arises with 'not'. We accounted for the fact that 'the *F* is not *G*' admits of more than one interpretation by saying that 'not' can operate on predicates or on completed sentences, but this does not show that 'not' is unambiguous. It will only be unambiguous if it operates *in the same way* when it operates on predicates and when it operates on completed sentences, that is, if the relation of 'Not($G(x)$)' to '$G(x)$' is the same as the relation of 'Not(p)' to 'p'. Now when is this so? It seems reasonable to understand these relations in terms of the extensions of the predicates – that is, what they apply to – on the one hand, and of the truth-values of the sentences on the other. That is, I think that we are justified in saying that the relation of one predicate to the other is the same as the relation of one sentence to the other, and thus that the same operator 'not' is involved in each case, because how the operator works can be specified as follows:

(i) by negating a predicate we form a predicate whose extension is complementary to the extension of the original predicate;

(ii) by negating a sentence we form a sentence whose truth-value is complementary to the truth-value of the original sentence.

In other words, the extension of the negated predicate has the same relation to the extension of the original predicate as the truth-value of the negated sentence has to the truth-value of the original sentence. This justifies us in saying that the same operation is performed in each case. To show that '*A* thinks that' is unambiguous we must similarly show that it works in the same way whether operating on predicates or on sentences. I think that this is so, because I think that we can specify how it works as follows:

(i) by prefixing '*A* thinks that' to a predicate we form a predicate having the extension which *A* in effect assigns to the original predicate;

(ii) by prefixing '*A* thinks that' to a sentence we form a sentence having the truth-value which *A* in effect assigns to the original sentence.

If these formulations are correct, then the operator '*A* thinks that' is the same whether applied to predicates or to sentences, but they are not as they stand particularly informative or self-justificatory. To show them to be reasonable, we must return from philosophical logic to the philosophy of mind. If belief itself can be looked at from two points of view, we can then understand why sentences employing '*A* thinks that' or '*A* believes that' should admit of two interpretations. I shall try to show that a plausible substantive account of belief accords with the above formulations. In this way philosophy of mind and philosophical logic interconnect and lend support to one another.

4

There are two ways in which one could approach the notion of belief. I shall outline them without pursuing them in any great detail.

(1) One could approach belief by considering a hypothetical creature, supposing it to behave in more and more complex ways, and asking what features its behaviour would have to display before it could be allowed to have beliefs or make judgements.[2] As Bennett points out, a creature can have beliefs without being a language-user. We talk of a dog thinking that it is about to be fed, or taken for a walk, and there is no reason to reject this as unwarranted anthropomorphism.[3]

An animal's beliefs or judgements are confined to particular items or the particular present or immediately future situation. An animal has a belief or makes a judgement if it classifies a particular item or situation in a certain way. If it lacks language, it can only do this if it has an appropriate behavioural response to items or situations for which it has evidence that they are of the kind in question. The animal can be said to classify an item or situation in a certain way if it responds appropriately to the item or situation. (Further conditions are necessary, for example that the animal must not behave as it does fortuitously, but because that behaviour is the appropriate response; these can largely be neglected in the present context.) Thus a dog can be said to think that a walk is imminent if it responds to a stimulus – e.g. its master reaching for a leash – of a kind which in its past experience has been followed by a walk, and if it re-

[2] Cf. Bennett's method in *Rationality*.
[3] Bennett, *Rationality*, §1.

sponds in the way it does because of the association in its past experience.[4]

An animal's concern is confined to the here and now, and the kinds of classification it can make are limited. One cannot say that animals assign to categories more specific than those for which they have particular behavioural responses. Thus one can only say that a dog specifically believes there is meat in the offing rather than that there is food in the offing if it has responses to meat-portending situations which it does not display in other food-portending situations. With language comes the possibility of classifying the absent, for one can classify a thing by characterising it, and one can characterise a thing, one can talk about it, even if it is not present to one.

Bennett claims that language is necessary for having beliefs, or making judgements, which are not about particular items or situations. This claim has been challenged by Kirk.[5] Kirk describes a race of solitary, non-communicating creatures which he refers to as Cyclopes, and whose behaviour an observer would be forced to describe as constructing experimental models to test universal hypotheses. But even if we have to concede that Cyclopes, although without language, have general beliefs, this need not present a very serious challenge to Bennett's position. The Cyclopean behaviour which leads us to say that they have general beliefs is importantly similar to linguistic behaviour. For to make a model is to use one thing or situation to stand for or represent a class of things or situations, and is thus really a form of symbolic behaviour, even if not linguistic. Bennett could reformulate his claim and say that some kind of symbolic behaviour is necessary for having general beliefs.

(2) Alternatively, one could approach belief from the human point of view, and think of it primarily in terms of assent to statements or propositions. Of course mere verbal assent to a statement is not sufficient for belief. One might say that the assent must be sincere, but whether this is helpful depends on how it is understood. Taken one way it would beg the question, for sincere assent might mean believing assent – someone's assent would be sincere if he believed what he was assenting to.

Some independent criterion for sincere assent would therefore be needed. The most hopeful possibility would seem to be to tie

[4] For further elaboration, see Bennett, *Rationality*, §4.

[5] R. Kirk, 'Rationality without Language', *Mind*, LXXVI (1967).

sincere assent, and thus belief, to non-linguistic behaviour, by means of the notion of practical argument or deliberation. Practical deliberation is deliberation addressed to the question of what to do. I shall say that a genuine practical deliberation is one which does actually affect behaviour. It is not enough to go through the moves mentally. What distinguishes genuine practical deliberation from mere shadow-play is its behavioural effect. Now any practical deliberation proceeds from certain premisses, some of them factual, some evaluative. We could therefore say that someone sincerely assents to the statement that p, and thus believes that p, if he would genuinely practically argue from the premiss that p.

5

I have suggested that the notion of belief can be approached in either of two ways. Beliefs can be attributed to a creature on the basis of its interactions with particular items in the world. Or beliefs can be attributed to a creature on the basis of its linguistic behaviour. It should be clear that these two ways of approaching belief correspond to the two suggested interpretations of sentences employing 'think' or 'believe'.

(1) If one approaches belief from the point of view of the classifications an animal can make, it is natural to understand belief statements extensionally. In the pre-linguistic situation, what is at issue is a creature's behavioural response to a thing or situation. Any statement reporting that the creature responds to a thing or situation, and any statement which is to be spelt out in terms of such behavioural responses, will be true whatever description is chosen. Substitutivity should therefore hold. The same is true when linguistic characterisation is considered. If A characterises B in a certain way, and $B=C$, then A characterises C in that way.

The particular formulation I gave was as follows:

(i) by prefixing 'A thinks that' to a predicate we form a predicate having the extension which A in effect assigns to the original predicate.

The 'in effect' serves to loosen the tie with the particular language whose formation rules are being stated. A predicate such as 'red' belongs to a particular language. But a creature can be said to think that something is red even if it does not speak English, indeed, even if it is not a language-user at all. One way of classifying something as red is to characterise it as 'red', but there are other procedures which are tantamount to this. Thus a creature can apply to the thing a predicate which means for it what 'red' means in English, or can classify it non-linguistically by behaving in an appropriate way. The extension of the predicate '*A* thinks that (red(*x*))' is thus not simply the extension which *A* assigns to 'red(*x*)', but the extension determined by any procedure equivalent to this, linguistic or non-linguistic. (The 'assigns' must, of course, be understood dispositionally.)

(2) If one approaches belief from the point of view of assent to statements, then it is natural to understand belief statements intensionally. Statements employ descriptions or proper names to refer to things, and someone could quite well sincerely assent to one statement employing one description or name, and sincerely dissent from another statement employing another description or name which in fact refers to the same thing. Thus to take Quine's example again, someone who is unaware that Cicero is Tully may assent to 'Cicero denounced Catiline', but dissent from 'Tully denounced Catiline'.

The particular formulation I gave was as follows:

(ii) by prefixing '*A* thinks that' to a sentence we form a sentence having the truth-value which *A* in effect assigns to the original sentence.

Once again the 'in effect' serves to loosen the tie with the particular language whose formation rules are being stated. Someone can be said to think that *p* if he assents to some statement which means for him what '*p*' means in English. Thus a Frenchman's assenting to 'Il fait froid' is equivalent to an Englishman's assenting to 'It is cold', and he will count as in effect assigning the truth-value *T* to 'It is cold'.

I have given what is merely a sketch of how an account of belief could be undertaken, but I think that it is sufficient to show how a discussion in the philosophy of mind can support a position in philosophical logic. I outlined a theory of belief statements according to which such statements can be interpreted in either of two ways. This theory can account for the relevant linguistic facts, the facts about our actual use of belief statements. But there may well be other possible theories of belief statements which are also consistent with the linguistic facts. That is, there may be alternative ways of ordering and systematising the linguistic data. To decide between these, appeal must be made to the substantive area which corresponds to the class of statements in question, in this case to the account to be given of belief itself. I have claimed that the way belief should be treated substantively, the existence of two viable approaches to the analysis of belief, accords with my account of belief statements as systematically ambiguous.

6

I shall deal briefly with certain outstanding points. I have suggested that a statement of the form 'A thinks that the F is G' can be understood either extensionally, as saying that A classifies the F in a certain way, or intensionally, as saying that A assents to a statement tantamount to 'the F is G'. To ask what the relation is between these two interpretations is to ask when a person, in assenting to a statement, is characterising a particular object, and is thus to raise the issues concerning reference which were discussed in Chapter xiv. I have discussed belief statements only, but there are other types of P_2-statements, such as reports of desires, which, if I am correct, will admit of a double interpretation along similar lines. A statement of the form 'A wants to see the F' will also admit both of an extensional and of an intensional interpretation. Clearly the relation between the interpretations will be systematic, that is, one interpretation of 'A wants to see the F' will bear the same relation to the other as one interpretation of 'A thinks that the F is G' bears to the other.

In Chapter xvi, 4, I raised the question of the parochiality of the discussion of P-statements. I asked whether we were just concerned with facts about certain statements in English, or whether there was reason to expect statements serving the same function in any other language to be relevantly similar. Insofar as the double interpretation of P_2-statements is rooted in the philosophy of mind, there do seem to be grounds for thinking that this ambiguity is not merely a parochial feature of the English language.

In the same section I asked the further question, why, if a statement like 'Smith believes that the mayor of Cambridge is in the next room' admits of two interpretations, we are not normally in doubt as to how to take it. On one interpretation it entails that there is someone who is the mayor of Cambridge, and substitutivity holds. On the other, it does not entail that there is someone who is the mayor of Cambridge, and substitutivity does not hold. In fact we often take such a statement in a way which corresponds to neither of these interpretations. Someone who uttered the statement would normally be taken to imply both that there is someone who is the mayor of Cambridge, and that Smith would accept this description of him, i.e. that he would assent to 'The mayor of Cambridge is in the next room'. I think that this can be explained if an apparently plausible principle governing discourse is valid, namely that someone who utters a statement which is dangerously ambiguous – i.e. which admits of two interpretations, such that it is true on one and false on the other – is under an obligation to qualify the statement in some way to make clear how it is to be understood. Correspondingly someone who utters an ambiguous statement without such qualification implies that the ambiguity is not dangerous, i.e. that the statement is true taken either way. Now 'Smith believes that the mayor of Cambridge is in the next room' will only be true on either interpretation if there is someone who is the mayor of Cambridge, and if Smith knows that this description is true of that person. Hence someone who utters this statement without qualification will imply that there is someone who is the mayor of Cambridge and that Smith would accept that description of that person, even though the statement itself admits of two interpretations neither of which carries both these implications.

I have argued that any $P2$-statement admits of two standard interpretations. Earlier I claimed that $P1$-statements, which assign objects to emotions and attitudes, can be given a basically extensional account. Why should these two classes of statement differ? The explanation is once more to be sought in the philosophy of mind. I suggested that there are two viable approaches to the analysis of belief, which give rise to two different ways of interpreting belief statements. But the account I gave of emotions treated them simply as concerns with or reactions to particular items in the world. On this account, we would expect statements assigning objects to emotions to be extensional.

Suppose that someone approached emotions from a different point of view, namely from the point of view of assent to utterances. He might, for instance, treat fear as a kind of assent to an utterance of the form 'The F is dangerous'. In this case he might then be

inclined to allow an intensional interpretation to emotion statements. But whether or not his alternative account was viable would
have to be settled at the level of philosophy of mind. Deciding how
emotion statements are to be interpreted would wait upon a decision
at the substantive level. Here, as elsewhere, the philosophy of mind
has priority.

XIX

Conclusion

I

To conclude, I would like to summarise what I have said, to relate my discussion to the more general themes raised in the opening chapter, and to suggest what seems to me to be a fruitful line of further investigation.

Two reasons have in the past been given for rejecting in principle a causal account of the emotion:object relation. I tried to show that neither is valid. The first is that the relation between an emotion and its object is non-contingent, and hence cannot be causal, for causal relations are contingent relations. I argued that the notion of a non-contingent relation rests upon a confusion. The second is that the nature of a person's knowledge of the objects of his own emotions rules out a causal account of what is known. I argued that a causal account can be reconciled with the facts about first-person knowledge, and furthermore that the type of causation prevalent in the mental sphere is no different from that prevalent in the physical sphere. Having shown that there is no reason in principle why the emotion:object relation should not be analysed causally, I attempted to outline a causal analysis.

The general notion of an object of emotion is a philosophical extension of everyday speech, and as such requires a rationale. I argued that Kenny's explanation of the notion in terms of logico-grammatical features of reports of emotions is unsatisfactory, not only in its particular details, but as a matter of principle. Such an approach, here, as elsewhere in the philosophy of mind, cannot provide a substitute for a substantive account. A rationale for the notion of an object must be given at a substantive level.

The term 'object' is sometimes used in such a way that the object of an emotion need not exist. I rejected this usage. Instead I restricted 'object' to items existing in the world. I took as my starting-point a person in relation to the world, rather than a mind in isolation, and asked when a person's concern with an item can be called emotional, and what has to be true for the item to be the object of the person's emotion. I claimed that for an item to be the object of someone's emotion, it must be causally involved in a certain way in the production of an emotion in that person. The causal link between object and emotion passes through thought or perception. In the case of perception, the causal chain is fairly straightforward. In the case of thought, it is more complex. If an emotion is caused by thought about the object, it is thought about the *object* only if the object played a certain part in the genesis of a dossier on which the thought draws. But for object-terminology to be in place, it is not sufficient that an item be causally involved in the production of an emotion. In addition the emotion must have a further relevance to the item of a kind I tried to describe.

Emotions typically arise from the apprehension of certain characteristics in the object, and involve certain tendencies or impulses to behave in regard to the object. Some such regular concatenations of perception and response have biological roots, some cultural. That we possess a common stock of emotional responses helps to explain our mutual comprehensibility.

Not all emotions have objects, for not all occur in the appropriate way in the interaction of people with items in the world. Some lack objects because they arise from a mistaken existential belief. Some are of the type I described as propositional. Such objectless emotions are nevertheless intentional. They can be said to have content, where this is understood in a non-relational way. Intentionality is a feature also of many other types of mental states, acts and dispositions, though not of all. Sensations are not intentional – thus Kenny correctly contrasts them with emotions. The fact that mental states are intentional cannot be used, however, to show that the mental is irreducible to the physical.

Although an account of intentionality should not be given in terms of logico-grammatical features of statements reporting intentional states, such statements do raise problems of interpretation. I tried to show that a satisfactory account of these statements must accord with what is said in the relevant area of philosophy of mind. If statements reporting beliefs admit of more than one interpretation, for example, it is because belief itself can be viewed in more than one way.

2

In the first chapter I outlined two commonly accepted accounts of the difference between men and other things, each describing it as a radical difference of kind. The Cartesians locate the difference in man's possession of a mind, or mental states, for they deny that the mental can be reduced to the physical. The neo-Wittgensteinians see man as in some way eluding the causal network in which physical things are enmeshed. Causal notions and causal explanations, they say, are not universally applicable to the human realm.

With these accounts we can contrast a third view, which sees the difference between men and other things, not as an irreducible difference of kind, but as a difference of complexity of organisation. According to this view, man is composed of the same ultimate constituents as other things. Men perceive, and think, and feel, and inanimate objects do not, but perceptions, thoughts and feelings are nothing but complex physical phenomena. Man's behaviour and his interactions with other things are fully covered by causal laws. This does not preclude the explanation of human action in terms of reasons and cognate notions, but is rather a precondition for such explanation. I shall call this view materialism, although its most tenable version is a synthesis of those views traditionally called materialism and behaviourism.

The anti-materialist schools cite intentionality in evidence. On the one hand, it is argued that the mental is intentional and the physical is not, hence that the mental cannot be a form of the physical. On the other hand, it is argued that intentional states such as emotions are related to their objects in a non-causal way, hence that this aspect at least of the interaction between men and the world escapes the causal network. I tried to show that the appeal to intentionality supports neither case.

But neither account stands or falls with the argument from intentionality. This book has been of more general relevance to the neo-Wittgensteinian view, whose case is primarily a negative one. The neo-Wittgensteinians claim that human behaviour and experience fall under a set of concepts, and admit of a kind of explanation, which are not causal, and which are inconsistent with causal explanation. They support this claim with *a priori* arguments, most of which belong to the same family as those I criticised in the context of the emotion: object relation. To show, for example, that explanation of behaviour in terms of a desire is not causal, it is said that a desire is non-contingently connected with its manifestation in behaviour, and that the nature of a person's knowledge of his own reasons for action rules out a causal analysis. My discussion may have helped to supplement the work of philosophers such as Davidson and Pears in demonstrating the invalidity of these negative arguments.

Materialists claim that the concepts we apply to human behaviour and experience can be analysed causally. To refute the *a priori* objections to this claim is not enough. There remains the constructive task of substantiating the claim by the production of causal analyses. I have tried to show in this book that the concept of an object of emotion is a causal concept. This, however, is only a small part of the total programme.

It should be clear what is involved here. Materialists do not deny that we need a special set of concepts to think about human experience and action, concepts inapplicable to inanimate objects. They do not claim that explanation in terms of reasons could ever be superseded by some other form of explanation. To say that a concept is causal is to say that it has application by virtue of a pattern in the causal network.[1] Such a concept applies if and only if a particular causal pattern is present, but how the pattern is made concrete may differ on different occasions, just as different materials can conform to the same pictorial pattern or design. Thus to say that the concept of a reason for action is a causal concept does not imply that when two people act for the same reason, the same underlying causal story can be told. There is no substitute for the concept of a reason, no other way of handling intellectually that particular kind of pattern in the causal network. Human behaviour cannot be understood and explained except by reference to reasons, desires, emotions, and the like, and to the interpretations which individuals put upon their own actions and the situations in which they act. A causal view lends no support to the equation of understanding with subsumption under general laws.

[1] See Chapter ii, 2.

3

Materialism faces a much more formidable enemy on its other flank. Little that has been said in this book is of direct relevance to the Cartesian view. The Cartesian case is not just a negative one. It is a view which appeals to reflective common sense. What goes on when someone thinks or feels or perceives does seem to be altogether different from physical phenomena. For a start, something does surely actually happen, which cannot be analysed away into dispositions to behave. But what happens seems to be irreducibly non-physical. One has a strong intuitive feeling that while the phenomena of consciousness such as thought and perception may be causally dependent on physical phenomena, they are not identical with those phenomena, but could conceivably exist in isolation. Looking at it from a first-person point of view, my physical body and its states seem in a sense accidental to my being. It seems to me that *I* could go on though my physical body ceased to exist. The idea of personal survival after death may in the end be incoherent, but it is clearly a widely held belief. Thus materialism seems to be opposed here not just to an important philosophical school, but to common sense.

The anti-materialists are not moved only by intuitive conviction and a desire to establish man's uniqueness, but by a belief that the most important aspects of our dealings with our fellow-men and of the way we view one another are threatened by materialism. Our moral interactions with our fellows are predicated on the assumption of responsibility and of free will, and such an assumption is thought incompatible with a view of man as a wholly material being, fully subject to causal laws. Why then should the materialist programme appear attractive? The materialist is seized by the scientific urge to simplify the universe. His universe is ontologically simpler, for it contains fewer fundamental types of constituent. It is simpler also in that causal interaction between the mental and the physical poses no problem. Nor need any worrying discontinuities be supposed in the evolution of man from inanimate matter.

The materialist can proceed in two directions. He can attempt to reduce the mental to the physical. Alternatively, he can attempt to show how the physical can be built up into the mental, and this may be the more hopeful strategy. He can start with something that is clearly the other side of the line, lacking those features which distinguish humans, and by a progressive series of complications, but without introducing any non-causal principles of organisation, try to approach as closely as possible to an analogue of man. This is the type of method that Bennett adopts in *Rationality*, but the bees with which he starts already possess some of the attributes of consciousness such as perception, and are thus really the wrong side of the line for our purposes. It is better, perhaps, to indulge in *a priori* robotology.[2] One can consider a machine which is capable of classifying and storing information, and allow it to behave in more and more complex ways, all, however, in principle explicable in causal terms. Does it eventually become reasonable to apply to it concepts analogous to those of perception, belief, desire, etc? More strongly, does it eventually become impossible to account for the machine's behaviour except in terms of such concepts? And if so, what is the difference, if any, between the concepts applicable to man and their supposed analogues applicable to the robot?

Such a procedure can shed light on the structure and interrelation of the particular concepts we apply to people, as well as on the general question of the nature of consciousness. I shall not attempt to carry out the programme in a rigorous way. Instead I shall use this method of approach to show how central the category of feeling is to our idea of what makes us distinctively human.

4

It is not difficult to imagine a machine which monitors the world, which stores information, and which processes that information to arrive at new information or putative information.[3] It can, for example, generalise from particular 'experience'. It can form 'theories' as to how the world works and as to the probable results of its actions, and can modify and correct these in the light of subsequent events – it can 'learn'. We can suppose it to have the power of locomotion and of manipulation of objects, and to behave in the

[2] Some of Hilary Putnam's work may be relevant here. See, for example, 'Minds and Machines', in S. Hook (ed.), *Dimensions of Mind* (New York, 1961).

[3] It must be allowed to operate according to probabilistic principles, and thus sometimes to arrive at a mistaken conclusion.

light of the information and theories it possesses to attain certain ends. The application of teleological categories to the machine presents no difficulty. That is, we can attribute to it ends of behaviour or goals, even if not purposes or intentions. We can suppose that it has been programmed to perform certain specific tasks, once for all or recurrent, and also to pursue general ends, like keeping itself sufficiently charged with energy and preserving itself from injury. We can also suppose it programmed to indulge in 'scientific' behaviour, to 'hunt' in a random or systematic way so as to increase its store of information and improve its theories as to how the world works. It might be endowed with a 'linguistic' capacity, able to print out reports on what it was monitoring, on information stored, on operations performed on that information, on behaviour and the ends towards which that behaviour was directed, and so on.

I do not know how much of this is technically possible, but it is quite conceivable. One can easily imagine a machine to which analogues of the concepts of perception, of belief, of ratiocination and theory-construction, of behaviour, of ends of behaviour, of learning, and of language can be applied. Nevertheless the machine as described still seems far from an adequate analogue of man, nor is it clear that we would yet be prepared to attribute consciousness to it, or to admit it to our side of the line. It is instructive to examine the ways in which it seems deficient, for these help to bring out the importance of the category of feeling.

The machine's behaviour can be said to be directed towards ends, but for several reasons this is insufficient to make it an analogue of man.

(1) The machine's behaviour conforms entirely to a means-end pattern. Whatever it does is done in pursuit of some specific goal, and is chosen out of the alternatives available to it on the grounds of efficiency as a means, as suggested by previous 'experience'. By contrast much human behaviour does not fit happily or naturally into a means-end pattern. Much of what we do is not dictated by any purpose which goes beyond the immediate situation. We do things because we like doing them, or because they suddenly take our fancy. We engage in undirected interaction with others, casually conversing, responding to what others do. We express our feelings, we act on whims and impulses, we fidget and fill in time, we get distracted from one occupation and start doing something else. If you observe what a person does over a period of time, a great deal

of it cannot really be described as goal-directed.[4] Much of our thought is similarly undirected and inconsequential. Even when a person's behaviour is directed towards an end, considerations other than efficiency and economy of effort usually enter into the choice of means. When going somewhere, we don't always take the shortest route, and the incidental activities we indulge in on the way, the whistling and kicking stones and plucking twigs from the hedgerow, dominated by its ends. It is as typically inconsequential as purposive, and when it is purposive the purpose dictates the broad outline of what is done rather than the specific manner in which it is done.

(2) The machine's behaviour is not autonomous, for its ends of action are set for it from outside. These ends are few in number, and persist from situation to situation. They do not arise out of the situations in which the machine finds itself, but are brought by it to these situations. The machine can acquire new ends as inter- are irrelevant to the main goal. Our behaviour, in other words, is not mediate steps towards the achievement of its original goals, when it 'learns' by 'experience' that these are necessary, but apart from this its ends can only be changed or added to through external inter- ference. A person's ends of action are to a certain extent determined by biological and social factors, but they are not in the same way imposed from outside. Within the limits that biology and society allow, people decide for themselves what they will try to achieve. Any person has a tremendous variety of ends of action. Some of these are persistent or recurrent, like the advancement of his career or the satisfaction of his bodily needs. Some are highly specific to

[4] Practically any action *can* be described in means-end terms. Instead of saying that someone did something because he liked doing it, one can say that he did it as a means to enjoyment. I think that this is a purely verbal manoeuvre, and that doing something because you like doing it, or because it expresses your feelings, is importantly different from the standard case of doing something as a means to a further end. It is not easy to show this briefly, for the distinction between an action and its consequences is a blurred one. However I think that a workable criterion for marking off genuine cases could be devised along the following lines: an action is done as a means to an end only if it is done because of its likely causal instrumentality in bringing about some further state of affairs. If I do something because I like doing it, or because it expresses my feelings, what I do is not, or at least need not be, intended as a contribution to the causal production of some further state of affairs.

particular situations, arising out of the person's experience of the situations themselves. People frequently change their minds, both about short-term and about long-term ends.

(3) The machine's behaviour has some coherence, for it can act at different times in pursuit of the same goal. But the various ends that the machine pursues do not in themselves form a coherent system. If they relate to one another, it is only through their common external imposition. The totality of a person's behaviour and of his ends of action does have a kind of coherence. There are two distinct ways in which different things that a person does can form a coherent whole. As with the machine, different actions can add up to a single complex of behaviour because they are all directed to the same end. But different actions can also be part of a unified whole because they all arise from the same feeling or attitude.[5] This is a distinct type of principle of unity of behaviour. In general, a person's actions, and the different ends he tries to achieve, are brought into relation one with another mainly through the feelings and emotions he has in particular situations, and through his longer-term attitudes towards the things and people and institutions around him, and towards himself in relation to these. Consider, for example, the complex of behaviour that one person displays towards another over a period of time. This is not a random collection of actions, but exhibits a coherent pattern. The coherence comes, not from the fact that the complex of behaviour towards the other can be subsumed under a single end or set of ends, but from the presence of a fairly constant attitude towards the other. My behaviour towards a friend hangs together, not because I always relate to him in pursuit of the same end, but because I like him. Variations from the general pattern can be explained in terms of transient feelings. Similarly how a person behaves in a particular situation can be given coherence by reference to his feelings in that situation, rather than by reference to his ends. What he does adds up to a unified whole because it all arises out of his feeling of nervousness, say, or of depression. Thus human behaviour has a kind of unity and coherence which that of the machine lacks, arising out of the network of feelings and attitudes in which it is embedded.

[5] Bernard Williams argues illuminatingly for a similar position in his Bedford College Inaugural Lecture. See B. A. O. Williams, 'Morality and the Emotions', *Bedford College Inaugural Lecture* (London, 1965), esp. pp. 17–18.

5

These, then, are some of the factors that make the postulated machine seem so alien and inhuman, and to fall short of an adequate analogue of man. Its behaviour is uniformly consequential and goal-directed. Its ends of action dominate its behaviour, which is governed solely by the criterion of efficiency. It never dallies by the wayside. Its ends are not self-generated, nor can it discard them. They are imposed on it from outside. They do not relate together to form a coherent system, but each exists individually in isolation. By contrast, human action is autonomous, often inconsequential, is related loosely rather than tightly to its ends, and is embedded in a network of feelings and attitudes which give it unity and coherence.

What distinguishes human behaviour is not that it is goal-directed, but that it, and the goals towards which it is directed, make a kind of sense. When I say that what a person does makes sense, I do not mean that it is justified, but that it is comprehensible, in a way in which the machine's behaviour is not comprehensible. What a person does, or his goal in acting, is comprehensible only if it ultimately springs from his feelings and attitudes.[6] Only if the machine could be said to feel and have attitudes would its behaviour be similarly comprehensible, and would it approach to an analogue of man.

At a first stage, we can make sense of an action in relation to an end, or in relation to a feeling or attitude. But an end gives sense to behaviour only insofar as it makes sense itself. An end can be given sense by reference to a more distant or more general end. But it can also be given sense by its own relation to an emotion or attitude. Thus Tom's behaviour towards Dick makes sense as a means to hurting Dick, but this end, hurting Dick, itself makes sense as arising out of Tom's feeling of anger. I think that in the last resort we demand that all ends of action make sense in terms of feelings and attitudes. If someone's end or goal, that which he is trying to achieve by acting in a certain way, cannot be related to his feelings and attitudes, it seems incomprehensible. Suppose that Tom acts so as to promote Mary's interest. If this end of action exists

[6] It is a further condition for the action or goal to be comprehensible to *me*, that the feelings and attitudes should not be alien to me. See Chapter x, 3.

wholly in isolation, it does not make sense. It needs some context to give it sense. The sense-giving context may be Tom's feeling for Mary, that he loves her, or it may be that someone else for whom he cared entrusted Mary's well-being to him, but only if securing her interest is an end arising from his feelings and attitudes is it comprehensible.

The many feelings and attitudes that a person has themselves form a coherent whole, though not an entirely consistent one. A person may have many contradictory and conflicting attitudes and beliefs, and even in particular situations ambivalence and inconsistency of feeling is common. But such inconsistency exists within a larger coherence. A person's total outlook, the whole collection of his feelings and attitudes and beliefs and opinions and views as to what is and ought to be the case, his expectations of others and conception of himself, his notion of what life is all about and of what is worth striving for, makes sense as a network of interconnected items loosely strung together, not as a logically ordered, hierarchical, self-consistent system. The coherence it displays is more like that of a piece of music than that of a logical calculus. It is above all their orderliness and hierarchical nature that detaches the moral systems of philosophers from human reality.

It is characteristic of feelings and attitudes that they give rise to behaviour which is not utilitarian, not directed towards an end. If Tom loves Mary, his behaviour in her regard is not governed solely by utilitarian considerations. His love shows itself in expressive behaviour. It may also affect his behaviour in situations in which Mary is not explicitly involved. For example, in her absence, or after a row, he may be unable to concentrate on what he is supposed to be doing. If Tom's behaviour towards Mary were wholly utilitarian, we could not say that he loved her. Just as an action, or a failure to act, can be inconsistent with the attainment of an end, so an action, or a failure to act, can be inconsistent with a feeling or attitude. It is inconsistent with trying to get a job from a man if I am rude to him, or with trying to pass my exams if I fail to work. Similarly it is inconsistent with gratitude towards a person if I harm his interests unnecessarily, or with love for someone if my behaviour is unaffected by her misfortunes, even if I cannot myself do anything to help her.[7] In this

---

[7] Of course in any particular case there may be an explanation for an apparent inconsistency between behaviour and end or feeling. The point is that there is a conflict which demands a specific explanation.

way feelings must give rise to non-utilitarian as well as to end-directed behaviour.

This bears on the notion of human rationality. A common view, which might be called utilitarian, conceives of the rationality of action in means-end terms. According to this view, the only really good kind of reason for doing something is one which relates to intended consequences. An action is rational only insofar as it is an efficient means to an end. If an action is non-utilitarian, if, for example, it expresses feeling, in a situation in which the expression of feeling has no utility, it is not rational. A rational man is one who always acts rationally. But if ends of action only make sense in a context of feelings and attitudes, and if feelings and attitudes necessarily give rise to non-utilitarian behaviour, this view of rationality must be inadequate, or at least inapplicable to the human situation. A rational man should surely be comprehensible. I don't think we could understand someone who aimed, let us say, to promote human happiness, if this end existed in isolation, and was not rooted either in a care or concern for other people, or perhaps in an attitude towards some supernatural being believed to have commanded it. Such feelings and attitudes would show themselves in behaviour which was not directly intended to promote happiness, for example in distress at others' misfortunes. If end-directed behaviour ultimately gets its sense from feelings and attitudes which also give rise to behaviour which is not end-directed, any adequate theory must allow rationality to both types of behaviour.

Feeling is not opposed to reason. On the contrary, the notion of feeling is central to human rationality. Feeling necessarily implies non-utilitarian behaviour. To the extent that someone approached the world like a calculating machine, guiding his behaviour wholly by reference to its likely consequences, conceiving of every action as a means to a specific end, we would be doubtful about saying that he felt anything at all. The utilitarian conception of rationality appears to ignore a whole dimension of human nature, the dimension of feeling, and in ignoring this, it ignores what makes people recognisably human. One might say that to be human consists not in conforming to the utilitarian model of means-end rationality, as some philosophers have claimed, but in departing from it. This is really to say that the model itself is deficient, that utilitarian man would be incomprehensible, and that a more generous conception of rationality is required.

A person's actions and his ends of action make sense, and form a coherent whole, because they are rooted in a complex network of feelings and attitudes. It is the organisation of human behaviour in *this* way, not the fact that it is directed to ends, that makes it seem distinctively human. A machine's behaviour may be goal-directed, but if it lacks a comparable organisation, the machine will fail to be an adequate analogue of man. Two questions remain. First, under what circumstances, if any, would we be prepared to allow feelings and attitudes to a machine? When would a machine's behaviour be comprehensible to us in the way that another person's behaviour is comprehensible? Secondly, is this kind of comprehensibility a necessary condition for consciousness? Could the machine as originally specified, whose behaviour wholly conformed to a means-end pattern, was not autonomous, and did not make sense in the way that a person's behaviour makes sense, nevertheless be conscious?

I shall not attempt to answer these questions, for I do not think that philosophical techniques alone can provide a final answer to them. The nature of the mind and of consciousness, the uniqueness and distinctiveness of human existence, the extent of individual responsibility and of free will, the development of machines which approximate more and more closely to men – these are problems to which work in many fields is relevant, from the growing mathematical study of Machine Intelligence to the empirical findings of sociologists and social anthropologists. When Descartes wrote, philosophy was not a distinct discipline, but was part of a general inquiry into the nature of reality. The specialisation of philosophy, its isolation from the mainstream of scientific investigation, has impoverished it, and has rendered it incapable of pursuing those problems which were once its central concern. As Quine has shown, problems cannot be divided sharply into the empirical and the conceptual. The study of human nature does not have two mutually irrelevant sides, one the province of philosophy, the other of the natural and social sciences, but is a complex field of overlapping problems, to whose solution philosophy and science must jointly contribute. The conceptual skills of philosophy are needed to answer the fundamental questions, but by themselves they are not sufficient. They can bear fruit only in the context of empirical inquiry.

Bibliography

Anscombe, G. E. M. *Intention*. Oxford, 1957.
  'The Intentionality of Sensation', in R. J. Butler (ed.), *Analytical Philosophy, II*. Oxford, 1965.
Bedford, E. 'Emotions', *Proceedings of the Aristotelian Society*, LVI (1955–6).
Bennett, J. F. *Rationality*, London, 1964.
  Kant's Analytic. Cambridge, England, 1966.
Casey, J. *The Language of Criticism*. London, 1966.
Chisholm, R. M. 'Sentences about Believing', *Proceedings of the Aristotelian Society*, LVI (1955–6).
  (ed.) *Realism and the Background of Phenomenology*. Glencoe, Ill., 1960.
Davidson, D. 'Actions, Reasons and Causes', *Journal of Philosophy*, LX (1963).
  'Causal Relations', *Journal of Philosophy*, LXIV (1967).
Descartes, R. *The Passions of the Soul*, in E. S. Haldane and G. R. T. Ross (translators), *The Philosophical Works of Descartes*. 2 vols., Cambridge, England, 1911. Vol. 1.
Findlay, J. N. *Values and Intentions*. London, 1961.
Gosling, J. C. B. 'Emotion and Object', *Philosophical Review*, LXXIV (1965).
Grice, H. P. 'The Causal Theory of Perception', *Aristotelian Society Supplementary Volume*, XXXV (1961).
Hume, D. *A Treatise of Human Nature*. Oxford, 1888.
Kenny, A. *Action, Emotion, and Will*. London, 1963.
Kirk, R. 'Rationality without Language', *Mind*, LXXVI (1967).
Melden, A. I. *Free Action*. London, 1961.
Murray, E. J. *Motivation and Emotion*. Englewood Cliffs, N.J., 1964.
Pears, D. F. 'Causes and Objects of some Feelings and Psychological Reactions', *Ratio*, IV (1962).
  'Are Reasons for Actions Causes?' in A. Stroll (ed.), *Epistemology*. New York, 1967.
  'Desires as Causes of Actions', in *The Human Agent, Royal Institute of Philosophy Lectures*, Vol. 1. London, 1968.
Perkins, M. 'Emotion and Feeling', *Philosophical Review*, LXXV (1966).
Pitcher, G. 'Emotion', *Mind*, LXXIV (1965).
Putnam, H. 'Minds and Machines', in S. Hook (ed.), *Dimensions of Mind*. New York, 1961.

'Brains and Behaviour', in R. J. Butler (ed.), *Analytical Philosophy II*. Oxford, 1965.

Quine, W. V. O. *From a Logical Point of View*. Cambridge, Mass., 1953.

Word and Object. Cambridge, Mass., 1960.

Ryle, G. *The Concept of Mind*. London, 1948.

Scheffler, I. 'On Synonymy and Indirect Discourse', *Philosophy of Science*, XXII (1955).

Taylor, C. *The Explanation of Behaviour*. London, 1964.

Teichmann, J. 'Mental Cause and Effect', *Mind*, LXX (1961).

White, A. R. *The Philosophy of Mind*. New York, 1967.

Williams, B. A. O. 'Morality and the Emotions', *Bedford College Inaugural Lecture*. London, 1965.

Winch, P. *The Idea of a Social Science*. London, 1958.

Wittgenstein, L. *Philosophical Investigations*. Oxford, 1953.

Zettel. Oxford, 1967.

Index